# STAGE DOOR

BY EDNA FERBER AND
GEORGE S. KAUFMAN

DRAMATISTS
PLAY SERVICE
INC.

## SIMPLIFIED ONE-SET VERSION OF THIS PLAY

*Stage Door* can with a few very minor changes be produced with one set only. Instructions as to the necessary minor changes appear at the back of the book. These instructions also include several textual changes which indicate simplification of settings, props and business and likewise suggest the omission of two small characters, Linda Shaw and Mrs. Shaw. Additional cuts indicated render the staging easier and exclude occasional bits of dialogue which might be considered a little "advanced" for the average high school.

# CAST OF CHARACTERS

Olga Brandt
Mattie (*colored maid*)
Young women
  Mary Harper (*Big Mary*)
  Mary McCune (*Little Mary*)
  Bernice Niemeyer
  Madeleine Vauclain
  Judith Canfield
  Ann Braddock
  Kaye Hamilton
  Linda Shaw
  Jean Maitland
  Bobby Melrose
  Louise Mitchell
  Susan Paige
  Pat Devine
  Kendall Adams
  Terry Randall
  Tony Gillette
  Ellen Fenwick

Mrs. Orcutt (*elderly woman*)
Frank (*colored houseman*)
Young men
  Sam Hastings
  Jimmy Devereaux
Business men
  Fred Powell
  Lou Milhauser
David Kingsley (*in the late thirties*)
Keith Burgess (*young man*)
Mrs. Shaw (*middle-aged woman*)
Dr. Randall (*middle-aged man*)
Larry Westcott (*publicity man*)
Billy (*photographer*)
Adolph Gretzl (*middle-aged man*)

## ACT I

Scene 1. The Footlights Club (Main Room). Somewhere in the West Fifties, New York.

Scene 2. One of the Bedrooms. A month later.

## ACT II

Scene 1. Again the Main Room. (Same as Act I, Scene 1.) A year later.

Scene 2. Two months later. (Same.)

## ACT III

Scene 1. The following season. (Same.) A Sunday morning.

Scene 2. About two weeks later. (Same.) Midnight.

# STAGE DOOR

## ACT I

SCENE 1: *The Footlights Club. A club for girls of the stage.*

*It occupies an entire brownstone house in the West 50's, New York. One of those old houses whose former splendor has departed as the neighborhood has changed.*

*The room we see is the common living room. It is comfortably furnished with unrelated but good pieces, enlivened by a bit of chintz. The effect is that of charm and livability, what with the piano, a desk, a fireplace with a good old marble mantel. Prominently hung is a copy of a portrait of Sarah Bernhardt, at her most dramatic. There is a glimpse of hallway with a flight of stairs. The lower part of the arch leading to hall is two low bookcases. The one L. stage holds the phone, the one R. stage holds mail, messages, papers, an occasional hat is thrown there.*

*It is an October evening, just before the dinner hour. The girls are coming home from matinees, from job-hunting, they are up and down the stairs, and presently they will be out again on dinner dates, playing the evening performances, seeing a movie.*

*Two girls are in the room at the moment, one at the piano up L., the other at a writing desk up R.*

*The girl at the piano, OLGA BRANDT, is dark, intense, sultry-looking. BERNICE NIEMEYER, at the desk, is a young girl definitely not of the ingenue type. This is at once her cross and [in her opinion] her greatest asset as an actress. For a moment nothing is heard but the music. The girl at the piano is playing beautifully, and with exquisite technique, Chopin's Nocturne in F Minor. A girl, SUSAN PAIGE, comes in from street door, stops for a quick look through the mail, tosses a "Hi!" into the room, and goes on up the stairs.*

*The piano again.*

5

BERNICE. (*To* SUSAN.) Hello. (*Rises, crosses to* OLGA.) What's that you're playing?

OLGA. (*Her Russian origin evident in her accent.*) Chopin.

BERN. How did you learn to play like that?

OLGA. Practice. Practice.

BERN. How long did it take you?

OLGA. (*Out of patience.*) Oh! (*A little discordant crash on the keys.*)

BERN. Well, I was just asking.

(*The phone rings as* MATTIE, *the maid, is descending the stairs, a little pile of towels over her arm.* MATTIE *is colored, about 30, matter-of-fact, accustomed to the vagaries of a houseful of girls, and tolerant of them.*)

MATTIE. Hello! Yes, this the Footlights Club. . . . (*To the girls in the room.*) Miss Devine come in yet? (*A negative shake of the head from* OLGA, *and a muttered "uh-uh" from* BERNICE.) No, she ain't. (*She bangs up.*)

BERN. (*To* MATTIE.) Was it a man?

(*Meanwhile voices are heard as street door opens.*)

BIG MARY. Oh no, let's have dinner here and go to a movie.

LITTLE MARY. Well, all right.

BERN. (*Pursuing her eternal queries.*) Who's that? (*Moves to* R. *of arch.*)

OLGA. (*A shade of impatience.*) Big and Little Mary.

(BIG *and* LITTLE MARY—MARY HARPER *and* MARY MCCUNE—*come into view in doorway from hall up* R. *There is a wide gap in stature between the two. One comes about to the other's elbow.*)

BIG M. What time is it? Dinner ready yet?

BERN. Where've you been? Seeing managers?

LITTLE M. (*Drooping.*) Yeh. We're dead.

(*The two* MARYS *in* C. *of arch.*)

BIG M. We've been in every manager's office on Broadway.

(OLGA *stops playing.*)

6

BERN. Is anybody casting?

BIG M. How do *we* know? We only got in to see *one* of them.

BERN. Which one? Who'd you see?

LITTLE M. Rosenblatt.

BERN. What's he doing?

BIG M. Take it easy. It's all cast. (*Her tone implies that this is the stereotyped managerial reply.*)

LITTLE M. All except a kid part—ten years old.

(BIG *and* LITTLE MARY *start upstairs.* OLGA *starts playing again.*)

BERN. (*Eagerly.*) I could look ten years old. (*She becomes a dimpled darling.*)

LITTLE M. No. Big Mary had the same idea, and she's littler than you are.

BIG M. You're almost as tall as Little Mary.

BERN. (*Crossing to* OLGA.) Listen, why is the little one called Big Mary and the big one Little Mary?

OLGA. (*Stops playing.*) Nobody knows. Will you for heaven's sake stop asking questions?

BERN. Oh, all right. . . .

MADELEINE. (*Enters* R.) Hello!

BERN. Where've you been? (*The last remark is addressed to a newcomer who stands in doorway. She is* MADELEINE VAUCLAIN, *a languid beauty, who runs through a sheaf of letters to discover if there is any mail for her. Phone rings.* BERNICE *picks it up.*) Footlights Club! . . . (*Another girl has come in street door and dashes upstairs pulling off coat as she goes up. She is* BOBBY MELROSE. BERNICE *to the girls.*) Terry Randall come in? (*As they shake their heads in negative.*) Not yet. (*Hangs up.*)

(OLGA *starts playing again.*)

MAD. (*Drops down* R. C.) I saw her sitting in Berger's office. I guess she gives up hard.

BERN. (*Alert at once.*) Is Berger doing any casting?

MAD. Listen, why don't you try making the rounds once in a while instead of sitting on your bustle and writing letters ——

BERN. (*Up the stairs.*) I make the rounds, but all you see is the office boys.

MAD. Well, who do you think sees the letters?

BERN. (*Stops on stairs a moment.*) Well, if they won't see you and won't read the letters, where do you go from there? (*Exit upstairs.*)

MAD. (*Calling after her.*) If you find out I wish you'd tell me.

MATTIE. (*In dining room doorway.*) Either you girls eating home?

MAD. I'm not.

MATTIE. Anyhow, it's ready. (*Goes, leaving doors open.*)

OLGA. (*Continues playing.*) Yes, yes.

MAD. Look, you don't want to go out tonight, do you? I've got an extra man.

OLGA. (*A shake of the head.*) I am rehearsing.

MAD. Tonight?

OLGA. (*With bitterness.*) Tonight. I play the piano for a lot of chorus girls to sing and dance. (*She goes into it, plays about eight bars of a very cheap tune, ends with discord. She rises furiously.*) That's what I am doing tonight—and *every* night! For that I studied fifteen years with Kolijinsky! (*Storms into dining room* L.)

MAD. (*Moves* L. *after her—mildly astonished at this outburst.*) Well, look, all I did was ask you if you wanted to go out tonight. (*A new figure appears in doorway. It is* JUDITH CANFIELD, *hard, wise, debunked. She has picked up a letter from hall table.*)

JUDITH. (*With dreadful sweetness as she drops down* C.) Oh, goody, goody, goody! I got a letter from home!

MAD. Hello, Judith!

JUD. (*Averting her gaze from letter as she opens it, brings herself to look at it with a courageous jerk of the head.*) Mmmm! Pa got laid off. (*Turns a page.*) My sister's husband has left her. (*Her eye skims a line or two. Turns another page.*) And one of my brothers slugged a railroad detective. I guess that's all. (*She moves* R. *to couch and sits.*) Yes. Lots of love and can you spare fifty dollars.

MAD. Nothing like a letter from home to pick you up. . . . Look, Judy, what are you doing tonight?

JUD. (*Who has dropped into a couch, whisked off her pump, and is pulling out toe of her stocking.*) I don't know. Why?

MAD. I've got an extra man.

JUDITH. (*Brightening.*) You mean dinner?

MAD. Yes. Fellow from back home in Seattle. He's in the lumber business. He's here for a convention.

JUD. Sounds terrible.

8

MAD. No, he isn't bad. And he's got this friend with him, so he wanted to know if I could get another girl.

JUD. Is the friend also in the lumber business?

MAD. I don't know. What's the difference!

JUD. He'll be breezy. " Hello, Beautiful! "

MAD. If we don't like it we can go home early.

JUD. Well—(*Weighing it.*) do we dress?

MAD. Sure!

JUD. Okay. I kind of feel like stepping out tonight.

MAD. (*Going toward stairs.*) Swell. We'd better start. It's getting late.

JUD. (*Tugging at her stocking.*) I'll be ready.

MAD. Hello, Ann.

ANN. Hello. (MADELEINE *disappears.* JUDITH *wriggles her cramped toes, sighs. Still another girl,* ANN BRADDOCK, *has come downstairs and goes toward dining room. She wears a hat and carries her coat, which she tosses onto piano as she passes.*) Going in to dinner?

JUD. Got a date.

ANN. Well, that's all right for you—you're not working. But I can't go out to dinner, and run around, and still give my best to the theatre. After all, you never see Kit Cornell dashing around. (*Righteously, she goes into dining room* L., *sits at head of table.*)

JUD. (*Mutters at first.*) Kit Cornell! (*Rises . . . Then raises her voice as portrait on wall gives her an idea.*) What about Bernhardt! I suppose *she* was a home girl!

(*From above stairs and descending stairway, the voice of* MRS. ORCUTT, *the House Matron, is heard.*)

MRS. ORCUTT. Yes, I'm sure you're going to be most comfortable here. Both of your roommates are lovely girls. Now if you'll just —— (*Sees* JUDITH.) Oh —— (MRS. ORCUTT *is a woman of about 46. In manner and dress you detect the flavor of a theatrical past. Her dress is likely to have too many ruffles, her coiffure too many curls. She is piloting a fragile and rather wispy girl whose eyes are too big for her face. We presently learn that her name is* KAYE HAMILTON.) Uh—this is Judith Canfield, one of our girls.—I'm so sorry, I'm afraid I didn't ——

KAYE. Kaye Hamilton.

MRS. OR. Oh, yes. Miss Hamilton is planning to be with us if everything—uh—she'll room with Jean and Terry, now that Louise is leaving.

9

JUD. That'll be swell. Excuse me. (*Shoe in hand, she limps toward stairs and up.*)

MRS. OR. (*A little gracious nod.*) Now, that's our dining room. (*A gesture.*) Dinner is served from six to seven, because of course the girls have to get to the theatre early if they're working. Now, let me see. You're in the same room with Terry and Jean, so that's only twelve-fifty a week, including the meals. I suppose that will be all right?

KAYE. Yes, thank you.

MRS. OR. Now, about the reference —— (*She looks at a piece of paper she has been holding.*) I'll have that all looked up in the morning.

KAYE. Morning? Can't I come in tonight?

MRS. OR. I'm afraid not. You see ——

KAYE. But I've got to come in tonight. I've got to.

(*A girl comes in at street door, runs through hallway and goes rapidly upstairs, humming as she goes: PAT DEVINE. Halfway up we hear her call: "Yoo-hoo!"*)

MRS. OR. (*After the interruption.*) Well—uh—it's a little irregular. However . . . Did you say your bags were near by?

KAYE. Yes. That is, I can get them.

MRS. OR. (*Reluctantly.*) Well, then, I suppose it's all right. . . . Now, we have certain little rules. As you know, this is a club for stage girls. I assume you are on the stage?

KAYE. Yes. Yes. I'm not working now, but I hope . . .

MRS. OR. I understand. . . . Now about callers—men callers, I mean ——

KAYE. There won't be any men.

MRS. OR. Oh, it's quite all right. We like you to bring your friends here. But not after eleven-thirty at night, and—of course—only in this room.

KAYE. I understand.

MRS. OR. I try very hard to make the girls feel that this is a real home. I was one of them myself not many years back, before I married Mr. Orcutt. Helen Romayne? Possibly you remember?

KAYE. I'm afraid I don't.

MRS. OR. That's quite all right. I think that covers everything. If you wish to go and get your bags —— Mattie! (*Peering toward dining room.*) Will you come here a minute?

10

MATTIE. (*In dining room.*) Yes, ma'am!

MRS. OR. (*She gently pilots* KAYE *toward doorway.*) Now, each girl is given a door-key and there's a little charge of twenty-five cents in case they're lost. So you see it's to your own interest not to lose it. Well, good-bye, and I'll expect you in a very short time. (*As* MATTIE *has appeared in dining room doorway* BERNICE *comes downstairs, crosses living room toward dining room.*)

BERN. What have we got for dinner, Mattie?

MATTIE. We got a good dinner.

BERN. (*As she disappears, sits on* ANN'S L.) Smells like last night. Is it?

(*Sounds of front door closing.* MRS. ORCUTT, *very businesslike, returns.*)

MRS. OR. Now, Mattie, there's a new girl coming in as soon as Louise Mitchell leaves. You'll only have a few minutes to get that room straightened up.

MATTIE. Yes, ma'am.

MRS. OR. Let's see, Terry Randall isn't in yet, is she?

MATTIE. No, ma'am.

MRS. OR. Well, if I don't see her be sure to tell her there's a new girl moving in with her and Jean. Don't forget fresh paper in the bureau drawers, and ——

(*Down the stairs like an angry whirlwind comes* LINDA SHAW, *clutching a dressing gown about her. Her hair is beautifully done, she is wearing evening slippers, obviously she is dressed for the evening except for her frock.*)

LINDA. (*Up* C.) Mattie, isn't my dress pressed yet?

MATTIE. (*Starting toward* LINDA.) Oh! Was you wanting it right away?

LINDA. Right away! When did you *think* I wanted it?

MATTIE. Well, I'll do it right this minute.

LINDA. Oh, don't bother! I'll do it myself! (*Storms out in hallway up* L.)

MATTIE. (*After her.*) You never give it to me till pretty near half-past five.

(*Phone rings.* MRS. ORCUTT *answers.*)

MRS. OR. I'll go. (*To* MATTIE *who exits up* L.) Footlights Club!
. . . Yes, she is . . . The Globe Picture Company? . . . Mr.
Kingsley himself? . . . Just a minute, (*Impressed*) I'll get her
right away. . . . (*Calls toward stairs.*) Jean! Oh, Jean!
JEAN. (*From above.*) Yes.
MRS. OR. (*In hushed tones.*) Mr. Kingsley of the Globe Picture
Company wants to talk to you.
JEAN. Oh, all right.
MRS. OR. (*Back to phone.*) She'll be right down. (*She lays down
receiver with a tenderness that is almost reverence, and takes a
few steps away, looking toward stairway. As* JEAN *appears,* MRS.
ORCUTT *affects an elaborate nonchalance and exits into dining
room.*)

(JEAN MAITLAND *is a beautiful girl in her early 20's. She is, perhaps, a shade too vivacious. A better actress off than on. Her hair
is blond, and that toss of her head that shakes back her curls is
not quite convincing. An opportunist: good-natured enough when
things go her way, she has definite charm and appeal for men.*
JEAN *throws her all into her voice as she greets the man at the
phone.*)

JEAN. Hello! Mr. Kingsley! How perfectly —— (*Obviously she
is met by a secretary's voice. Dashed by this, her tone drops to
below normal.*) Yes, this is Miss Maitland. Will you put him on,
please? (*Again she gathers all her forces and even tops her first
performance.*) Hello! Mr. Kingsley! How wonderful! . . . Yes, I
know you said that, but in your business you must meet ⌐ million
beautiful girls a day. . . . Well, anyhow, half a million. . . .
(*Coyly.*) . . . Dinner! You don't mean tonight! Oh! . . . Yes,
I did have, but it's nothing I can't break. . . . Oh, but I want to.
I'd love to. . . . What time? . . . Yes, I'll be ready. I suppose
we're dressing? . . . Yes, I'd love to. All right. Good-bye.

(*As she hangs up receiver, figures pop out of the vantage points
from which they have been listening.* BERNICE *and* ANN *come out
of dining room with* MRS. ORCUTT; *cloppity-clop down the stairs
come* BIG *and* LITTLE MARY *and* BOBBY MELROSE. BOBBY *is a soft
Southern belle, fluffy, feminine. At the moment she is in a rather
grotesque state of nettle hair-curlers, cold cream and bathrobe.*)

12

BIG M. (*A squeal of excitement.*) Jean!
BERN. I'm dying!
LITTLE M. Tell us all about it!
ANN. Yes, do!                                    (*Simultaneous.*)
BOBBY. What time is he coming?
MRS. OR. (*Entering.*) Well, Jeanie, does this
mean we're going to lose you to pictures?

(OLGA, *too, appears in dining room doorway, and stands there,
absorbing the scene.*)

BOBBY. Aren't you palpitating?
BERN. How soon is he coming? Can I see him?
JEAN. Now listen, you girls, no fair hanging around when he
comes.
LITTLE M. Aw!
JEAN. You've got to promise me—no parading.

(*The girls have come down* C.)

BIG M. Big-hearted Bertha!
BERN. I'll bet you'll let Terry meet him.
JEAN. Well, Terry's different.
ANN. All this fuss about a man! I wouldn't lift my little finger to
meet him. (*She stalks into dining room, sits head of table.*)
LITTLE M. She is over-sexed!
MRS. OR. David Kingsley! You know, he was Al Woods' office boy
when I played "The Woman in Room 13."
BERN. (*Off hand.*) Really? (*To* JEAN.) What are you going to
wear?
JEAN. I wonder if Pat'll let me have her rose taffeta.
BERN. Sure she would!
JEAN. And I'll wear Kendall's evening coat.
MRS. OR. When he became a producer he wanted me for his first
play. But by that time I had married Mr. Orcutt ——

(*From above-stairs comes the sound of singing: "Here Comes the
Bride." Other voices take it up. The group in the room at once
knows what this means, and their attention is turned toward
stairs.*)

13

BIG M. Oh, here's Louise!

BERN. Louise is going!

BOBBY. Oh, my goodness! I promised to help her pack!

LITTLE M. Let's get some rice and throw it!

BIG M. Oh, for heaven's sake, that's silly.


(ANN *enters* L. FRANK, *the houseman, comes downstairs laden with bags.* MATTIE'S *husband—35 or so. Close on* FRANK'S *heels comes* LOUISE MITCHELL *in traveling clothes, wearing a corsage of gardenias. She is accompanied by 3 girls. One is* SUSAN, *a student at an acting school. The others are* PAT DEVINE, *a night-club dancer, and* KENDALL ADAMS, *of the Boston Adams'.* MATTIE, *broadly grinning and anticipatory, comes to dining room doorway.* LOUISE *is ushered into room on a wave of melody.*)


MRS. OR. Well, my dear, and so the moment has come. But when you see how saddened we are, you will realize that parting is sweet sorrow, after all.


(JUDITH *comes downstairs, followed by* MADELEINE. *Both in deshabille.*)


JUD. (*As she drops down* R.) Well, Mitchell, you're finally getting the hell out of here, huh?

MRS. OR. Judith! That seems to me hardly the spirit.

JUD. Sorry.

LOUISE. Judy doesn't mean anything.

FRANK. (*In hallway.*) Shall I get you a taxi, Miss Louise?

LOUISE. Oh, yes, thank you, Frank. (FRANK *exits up* R. *with bags. The moment of departure has come. She looks about her for a second.*) Well, I guess there's no use in my trying to —— Why, where's Terry? I thought she was down here.

KENDALL. Isn't she here?

SUSAN. No.

JEAN. She hasn't come in yet.

LOUISE. Oh dear, I can't go without seeing Terry.

BERN. What's she up to, anyhow? I haven't seen her for days.

JEAN. I don't know. She's gone before I'm awake in the morning.

LOUISE. Well, anyhow, I guess I'd better get out of here before I bust out crying. You've all been just too darling for words, every single one of you —— (LINDA, *having retrieved her dress, flashes*

14

*through hall from up* L. *and makes for stairs.*) Who's that? Oh, good-bye, Linda. I'm going. (LINDA, *no part of this, tosses a " good-bye " over her shoulder as she goes upstairs.*) And no matter how happy I am, I'll never forget you, and thanks a million times for the perfume, Pat, and you, Susan, for the compact, and all of you that clubbed together and gave me the exquisite nightgown.

BERN. Oh, that's all right.

LOUISE. So—I hope I'll make a better wife than I did an actress— I guess I wasn't very good at that ——

BIG M. You were so!

KEN. Yes.

LITTLE M. You were swell!

LOUISE. I guess I wasn't *very* swell or I wouldn't be getting marr—(*Catches herself.*) that is, any girl would be glad to give up the stage to marry a wonderful boy like Bob—anyway, *I* certainly am. Goodness, when I think that for two whole years he's waited back there in Appleton, I guess I'm pretty lucky.

BIG M. Yes.

(*The faces about her, while attentive, do not reflect full belief in her good fortune.*)

LOUISE. Well, if any of you ever come out that way with a show, why, it's only a hundred miles from Milwaukee. Don't forget I'll be Mrs. Robert Hendershot by that time, and Wisconsin's perfectly beautiful in the autumn—the whole Fox River valley—it's beautiful —— (*It's no use. She cannot convince even herself, much less the rather embarrassed young people about her.*)

(*The situation is miraculously saved by the slam of the street door and the electric entrance of a new and buoyant figure.* TERRY RANDALL *has the vivid personality, the mobile face of the born actress. She is not at all conventionally beautiful, but the light in her face gives to her rather irregular features the effect of beauty. High cheekbones, wide mouth, broad brow.*)

TERRY. (*Breathless in hallway.*) LOUISE!

SUSAN. *Here's* Terry!

PAT. Where've you been?

TERRY. (*As she drops down* C. *to* LOUISE.) Dar-ling! I was so afraid you'd be gone. I ran all the way from Forty-sixth Street.

15

Nothing else in the world could have kept me—look—what do you think! I've got a JOB!

(*This announcement is greeted with a chorus of excited exclamations.*)

BOBBY. You haven't!
BERN. Who with?
PAT. Tell us about it!  } (*Simultaneous.*)
SUSAN. Terry, how wonderful!
BIG M. Tell us all about it!
TERRY. I will, afterward. . . . Louise, what a darling crazy hat! I just love it on you.
LOUISE. Oh, Terry, have you really got a job! What in?
JEAN. Who is it? Berger?
TERRY. Yes.
BERN. I thought he was all cast.
TERRY. He was, all except this one part. It's not big, but it's good. It's got one marvelous scene—you know—one of those gamuts. (*With three attitudes and a series of wordless sounds—one denunciatory, one tender, one triumphant—she amusingly conveys the range of the part.*)

(*From among the group:*)

SUSAN. It sounds marvelous!
PAT. Terry, you'll be wonderful!
FRANK. (*In hallway.*) Taxi's waiting, Miss Louise.
GIRLS. Oh!
LOUISE. (*A glance at her wrist-watch.*) Oh, dear, I can't bear to go. How'll I ever hear the rest of it? I've got to go ——
JEAN. Oh, dear.
GIRLS. Aw!
LOUISE. Terry, baby!
TERRY. Be happy, darling!

(LOUISE *throws her arms about* TERRY, *kisses her. General embracing and good-byes.*)

LOUISE. Jean! Kendall! (*She kisses* JEAN, *her other roommate.*)

16

Good-bye, good-bye! (LOUISE *is hurrying from room, others streaming into hallway to speed her.*)

KEN. Don't forget us!

MAD. Send us a piece of wedding cake!

JUD. We want the deadly details.

(*A chorus of good-byes from the girls.*)

MRS. OR. I hope you'll be very happy, dear child. Good-bye . . . good-bye . . . good-bye!

(LOUISE *is gone. The girls stream back into room.*)

KEN. When do you go into rehearsal, Terry?

OLGA. Yes, when?

TERRY. (*As she drops down* L. *to armchair.*) Right away!

BERN. Gosh, Terry, you certainly got a break. Berger wouldn't even talk to me.

LITTLE M. Berger's an awful meany. How'd you get to him, anyway?

TERRY. I just stood there outside his door for a week.

PAT. And it did the trick?

BIG M. *I* tried that.

BOBBY. It never helped *me* any.

JUD. Me neither. I laid there for a whole afternoon once with "Welcome!" on me.

TERRY. I've had a longer run outside his office than I've had with most shows. This was my second week. I was just going to send out for a toothbrush and a camp chair (*Rises.*) when suddenly he opened the door. He was going. I said, "Mr. Berger!" That's practically all I've said for two weeks—"Mr. Berger." (*She gives four readings of "Mr. Berger," ranging from piteous pleading to imperious command.*)

LITTLE M. What did he do?

SUSAN. What happened?

TERRY. He never even stopped. Suddenly I was furious. I grabbed his arm and said, "Listen! You're a producer and I'm an actress. What right have you got to barricade yourself behind closed doors and not see me! And hundreds like me! The greatest actress in the world might be coming up your stairs and you'd never know it."

KEN. Terry! What did he say!

TERRY. He said, "Are you the greatest actress in the world?" I said, "Maybe." He said, "You don't look like anything to me. You're not even pretty and you're just a little runt." I said, "Pretty! I suppose Rachel was pretty. And what about Nazimova! She's no higher than this." (*Indicates a level.*) "But on a stage she's any height she wants to be."

JUD. P. S. She got the job.

TERRY. Yes. (*A deep sigh that conveys her relief at the outcome.*) And when I walked out on Broadway again it seemed the most glamorous street in the world. Those beautiful Nedick orange stands, and that lovely traffic at Broadway and Forty-fifth, and those darling bums spitting on the sidewalk —— (*Doorbell rings. Instantaneously the group is galvanized. The girls realize the lateness of the hour.* TERRY *glances at her watch.*) Oh, my!

MAD. A suitor!

KEN. My word, it's late! (*Runs for stairs.*)

BIG M. Come on, let's eat.

(*To dining room with* LITTLE MARY, ANN, OLGA *and* BERNICE.)

BOBBY. Oh, it's my new young man. Mattie, tell him I won't be a minute. (*Dashes upstairs.*)

(*Meanwhile* MADELEINE *and* JUDITH *are dashing for stairs.*)

MAD. Wait a minute, Mattie. Give us a chance to get upstairs.

JUD. Yes, Mattie. We don't want to give him the wrong idea of this house.

JEAN. (*As she starts for stairs with* TERRY.) Terry, I couldn't be gladder.

TERRY. Me neither.

JEAN. Terry! What do you think's happened to your little girl friend? I'm having dinner with David Kingsley tonight.

TERRY. Jean, how marvelous! Did he say anything about a picture test?

JEAN. (*As they go upstairs.*) Not yet, but it must mean he's interested. Now look, when he gets here I want you to come down and meet him, because you never can tell.

(MATTIE, *having waited until the coast was clear, now goes to front door. Sound of a man's voice.* HASTINGS: "*Is Miss Melrose* in?" MATTIE's reply: "Yes, she is. Come right in." A young man stands in doorway, a trifle ill at ease in these unfamiliar surroundings. He hasn't the look of a New Yorker. There is about him the rather graceful angularity and winning simplicity of the Westerner.)

MATTIE. You-all can wait in there.
YOUNG MAN. Oh, thanks. Just tell her Sam Hastings is calling for her.
MATTIE. (As she goes to dining room door.) I think she knows about it—she'll be down directly.

(SAM HASTINGS mutters a thank-you as MATTIE passes into dining room, closing doors behind her. Left alone, and not yet at ease, SAM makes a leisurely survey of the room, rather getting in the way of his own big frame as he turns. He decides, unfortunately, on the least substantial chair in the room up L. and sits gingerly on its edge. At once there is a short sharp crack of protesting wood. He is on his feet like a shot. He prowls the room a bit. From above stairs a snatch of popular song. Swift footsteps are heard descending stairs. He turns expectantly but it's not his girl. It is KENDALL, who is humming a bit of song as she comes. Stops on stairs to fix stocking. She stops abruptly as she sees a stranger. With a glare at the embarrassed SAM she goes into dining room. Doorbell rings. Then a peremptory voice shouts from upstairs:)

JEAN. Judy. (Followed by three sharp raps on a door.) You going to stay in the johnny all night?

(He clears his throat and looks away, though there's nothing to look away from. BERNICE comes out of dining room. Closes door behind her. Her eye brightens as she beholds the young man.)

BERN. (Summoning all her charm.) Oh, pardon me. You're not Mr. David Kingsley!
SAM. No. My name's Hastings.

(With a syllable of dismissal, "Oh!" BERNICE goes on her way, and up the stairs. By this time MATTIE is opening front door. A voice [DEVEREAUX'] inquires:)

DEVEREAUX. Miss Paige in?

MATTIE. Yes, come right in. (*The boy who appears is even younger than* SAM. *Perhaps 19. Slight, graceful, dark-haired, rather sensitive looking.* MATTIE *calls from foot of stairs.*) Miss Susan!

(SUSAN'S *voice from upstairs—" All right, Mattie!"* MATTIE *exits up* L. *The two boys confront each other rather uncertainly. The newcomer in the doorway ventures a mannerly:*)

DEV. (*Over* L. C.) How do you do?

SAM. Howdy-do?

(*A little awkward pause.*)

DEV. My name's Devereaux.

SAM. Mine's Hastings.

DEV. Yes, I recognized you. I saw you in that Keith Burgess play last month.

SAM. (*Over* R.) You sure must have looked quick.

DEV. I liked that part. You did a lot with it. Too bad the play flopped.

SAM. I don't rightly recall you. Have you played anything lately?

DEV. Last month I played Emperor Jones, and I'm cast now for Hamlet.

SAM. Hamlet?

DEV. I'm at the New York School of Acting. This is my last year.

SAM. Oh! And then what?

DEV. Then I'm going on the stage.

SAM. Did you ever try to get a job on the stage?

DEV. Not yet.

SAM. That's more of a career than acting. I've been in New York two years. I'm from Texas. Houston Little Theatre. We came up and won a contest, and I stayed. I've had two weeks' work in two years. Don't ask me how I live. I don't know.

DEV. You could go back to Texas, couldn't you?

SAM. Go back! Oh, no! I'm an actor.

(SUSAN *runs down stairs, in street clothes.*)

SUSAN. Hello, Jimmy!

DEV. Hello, Sue. Do you know Mr. Hastings?

20

SUSAN. How-dy do?

DEV. Miss Susan Paige. She's up at the school, too. She's going to do Hedda Gabler.

SAM. Well, you have to start somewhere.

SUSAN. (*Laughingly.*) Yes.

(DEVEREAUX *says " Good-bye!" There is a word of farewell from* SAM *and* SUSAN *as doorbell rings.*)

DEV. (*As he and* SUSAN *go into hall.*) Where do you want to eat?

SUSAN. (*Going off up* R.) How much money have you got?

DEV. Sixty-five cents.

SUSAN. I've got thirty. That's ninety-five. (*As they open door they are accosted by a hearty masculine voice, subsequently identified as that of* FRED POWELL. *" This the Footlights Club? "*) Yes. Won't you just —— Mattie! Somebody at the door.

(MATTIE *having appeared in hallway.*)

MATTIE. Yes'm, Miss Susan. . . . You gentlemen calling on somebody?

(FRED POWELL *and* LOU MILHAUSER *come into view. They are two over-hearty Big Business men out for a holiday. Their derby hats and daytime attire will be a shock to the girls, especially* JUDITH.)

POWELL. Yes, we're calling for Miss Madeleine Vauclain.

MILHAUSER. And her friend.

MATTIE. (*At foot of stairs.*) Miss Madeleine!

MAD. (*Upstairs.*) Yes.

MATTIE. Couple gentlemen down here say they calling for you and —somebody.

MAD. Coming down!

MATTIE. She's coming down.

(*They come into living room, and finding another man there, offer a tentative greeting, a smile and wave of the hand. Then they look the room over.*)

MILH. What'd you say this place was? A Home for Girls?

POW. Yeh, all actresses. A whole bunch of 'em live here.

21

MILH. Kind of a handy place to know about.

POW. Yeah.

MILH. (*Whisks from his pocket two cellophaned cigars.*) Smoke?

POW. Thanks.

(*As they light up, MILHAUSER, having tossed crumpled cellophane jackets to a nearby table, sends a glance of half-inquiry at SAM. Hastily, in order to divert any further advances, SAM opens his cigarette case and lights a cigarette.*)

MILH. Certainly is a funny place, New York. Now, you take a lay-out like this. Wouldn't find it anywhere else in the world.

POW. Bet you wouldn't, at that.

MILH. I—I always thought actresses lived in flats or—uh—hotel rooms.

POW. Lot of 'em do.

MILH. (*Struck by a new thought.*) What about men actors—where do they live?

POW. I don't know—Lambs' Club, I guess.

MILH. Oh, yeah.

(*SAM shifts his position a little, throws them a look. BOBBY, finally coming down stairs, saves the situation. She is at her most Southern.*)

BOBBY. (*From stairs.*) Hello, there, Texas!

SAM. (*Gathering up his coat and hat.*) Oh, hello!

BOBBY. Ah hope Ah didn't keep you waitin'.

SAM. No! No!

BOBBY. One thing about me, Ah'm always prompt.

(*Outer door closes. They are gone off up R.*)

POW. That was a cute little trick.

MILH. Yeah. . . . Look! What about this one you've got on the fire for me? She any good?

POW. Sure, sure. You leave it to Madeleine.

MILH. Oh, well, as long as she's good-natured.

(*There is a rustle of silk on stairway. " Ah! " exclaims POWELL in anticipation and relief. MADELEINE and JUDITH descend stairs*) in full evening regalia, gathered from the richest recesses of the club—furs, silks, gloves, jewelry.)

MAD. (*Furiously, as she catches sight of the men's attire.*) Well, is this what you call dressing?
POW. Huh?
MAD. Why didn't you come in overalls!
POW. Now, now, baby. We got snarled up in a committee meeting, didn't we, Lou?
MILH. Sure. Sure.
POW. This is Lou Milhauser, girls. Miss Madeleine Vauclain and —uh ——
MAD. (*Sulkily.*) This is Miss Canfield.
MILH. Hello, Beautiful! (*Very jovial. He crosses to* JUDITH, *takes her arm.*) How about it? Shall we step out and go places?
JUD. Yes, let's.
MILH. Now, don't be like that. We're going to have a good time.
POW. Sure we are! The works! (*He is piloting* MADELEINE *out to hallway.*) Come on, boys and girls! Where do we want to eat?
MILH. (*As he starts off with* JUDITH.) I got an idea. How about a little Italian place?
JUD. Little Italian *nuts.* I want a decent dinner.

(*A slam at door. They are gone.*)

OLGA. (*Entering and speaking to* KENDALL *as latter enters living room from dining room.*) Kendall, are you going to your show? I am rehearsing at the Winter Garden, if you want to walk down. (OLGA *crossing to* C.)
KEN. It's too early for me. We don't go up till eight-fifty.

(*The* TWO MARYS *enter from dining room.*)

OLGA. The Winter Garden! The star pupil of Kolijinsky at the Winter Garden! (*She stalks out street door up* R.)
LITTLE M. Bellyaching! And she's got a job! Look at *me.* Edwin Booth and I retired from the stage at practically the same time.
KEN. (*As she starts for stairs.*) Oh, dear, I think I'll take a rest before the night show. Matinee days are frightfully tiring. (*She goes up to her room.*)

BIG M. Frightfully tiring! Why doesn't she go back to Boston. where she belongs! That'd rest her up.

LITTLE M. There ought to be an Equity law against society girls going on the stage. "Miss Kendall Adams, daughter of Mr. and Mrs. Roger Winthrop Adams."

BIG M. "Of Boston and the Lucky Strike ads."

(PAT and ANN come out of dining room. The tinkle of china and silver. The doors are shut by MATTIE. Dinner is over.)

ANN. What's it like out? It looked rainy when I came in.

BIG M. (At window.) No, it's all right. . . . Oh, girls, look! There's the Cadillac again for Linda Shaw.

LITTLE M. Is he in it?

BIG M. No, just the chauffeur, same as always.

PAT. Who's the guy, anyhow? Anybody we know?

LITTLE M. He doesn't ever come. Just sends the car.

PAT. Well, nice work if you can get it.

ANN. (Righteously.) I think it's disgraceful. A nice girl wouldn't want a man to send for her that way. And if you ask me, it gives the club a bad name.

(A warming gesture and a " pss-s-st!" from LITTLE MARY as LINDA descends stairs. LINDA is beautifully dressed for the evening. She is wearing the dress whose pressing had annoyed her, her evening cape is handsomely furred. Enormous orchids.)

BIG M. Oo, Linda! How gorgeous!

LINDA. (Pausing reluctantly.) Oh, hello.

LITTLE M. Come on in. Let's see you.

BIG M. What a marvelous coat, Linda!

PAT. Yes, and a very nifty bit of jack rabbit, if I may say so. (Her finger outlines a collar in the air.)

LINDA. Oh, that! Mother sent it to me. It used to be on a coat of hers.

LITTLE M. It's lovely.

PAT. (Mildly.) Oh—mother has a nice taste in orchids, too.

LINDA. Yes. Don't you wish you had a mother like mine? (She sweeps out.)

(The TWO MARYS dart to window.)

24

PAT. What would you two do without that window? Why don't you pull up a rocking chair?

ANN. Linda Shaw's comings and goings don't interest me. Girls make such fools of themselves about men! (*She goes out up* R.)

BIG M. Say, what do you know about Jean? Having dinner with David Kingsley.

LITTLE M. Some girls have all the luck. Where'd she meet him anyhow?

BIG M. Oh, at some cocktail party.

PAT. I wish I could meet him. He can spot picture material like that. He's got an eye like a camera.

LITTLE M. Yeah. He picked three stars last year. Nobody ever heard of them before he sent them out there.

PAT. (*Yawning and stretching.*) Well, *I'll* never meet him. . . . Oh, what to do till eleven o'clock! Except sleep.

LITTLE M. Anyhow, you've got something to *do* at eleven. . . . Look at us!

BIG M. Yeah, you're working.

PAT. I hate it. Hoofing in a night club for a lot of tired business men. The trouble is they're *not* tired and there's no business.

(*Doorbell rings.*)

BIG M. (*At window.*) I think it's David Kingsley! It looks like him.

PAT. Kingsley? Are you sure?

LITTLE M. (*Peering.*) Yes, that's him. Look, we'd better get out of the way, hadn't we?

BIG M. Yes, I guess so.

(PAT, *mindful of her pajamas, also gathers herself together.* BERNICE *runs down stairs with rather elaborate unconcern.*)

BERN. (*Too polite.*) Oh, pardon me, I just want to speak to— Frank—about—something —— (*Exits dining room.*)

(PAT *stands looking after* BERNICE *for a second. Then, as* MATTIE *crosses hallway to answer door* PAT *makes her own decision and darts up stairs. A man's voice at door.*)

KINGSLEY. (*In hall.*) Miss Maitland, please.

MATTIE. Yessuh. Come right in.

KINGS. Tell her, Mr. Kingsley. (DAVID KINGSLEY *enters. Perhaps 36 or 37. A man of decided charm and distinction, wearing evening clothes. You see his white muffler above the dark topcoat.*)
MATTIE. If you'll just rest yourself, Mr. Kingsley—I'll go right up. (MATTIE *goes up stairs with a stateliness that indicates her appreciation of the caller's importance.*)

(KINGSLEY *glances about the room a bit. He opens cigarette case, lights a cigarette.* BERNICE *comes out of dining room. Her face is turned toward someone in the room she has just left, and it is this person she is addressing, apparently all unaware that anyone, certainly not* KINGSLEY, *is in the living room.*)

BERN. Yes, Mattie, an actress's life is such an interesting one; if you could only see the different types that I do in the course of a day, Mattie. For example, an English actress came into an office today. (*Goes suddenly very English.*) "My dear Harry, how definitely ripping to see you. Definitely ripping!" And then, Mattie, a little girl from Brooklyn came in. "Listen, I did write for an appurntment! You got a noive!" (*She turns, and to her obvious embarrassment there is* MR. KINGSLEY. *She is a picture of pretty confusion.*) Oh, I am so sorry! I didn't dream anyone was here.
KINGS. (*Politely amused.*) That's quite all right.
BERN. (*Following up her advantage.*) I'm—Bernice Niemeyer. (KINGSLEY *bows slightly, murmurs her name.*) Well—I just thought —— (*She is dangling at the end of her rope.*)

(*Here she is mercifully interrupted by* PAT'S *descent of the stairs and singing. The jacket of* PAT'S *pajama suit is missing. Her slim figure is well revealed in the trousers and scant short-sleeveless top. Her low-heeled scuffs have been replaced by pert high-heeled mules.*)

PAT. I wonder —— (*Makes a slow turn toward* BERNICE—*a turn which by a strange chance serves at the same time to reveal the best points of her figure to the waiting* KINGSLEY.) You—you didn't see my book anywhere around here, did you?
BERN. (*Sourly.*) What book? (*She goes upstairs.*)

(PAT *flutters in her quest to a table, goes to bookshelf, selects a*

26

*volume, ruffles its pages to make sure the book meets her mood, then gives a little sigh of delight, clasps book to her breast and trips upstairs, turns to show her bare back and is off.* KINGSLEY *barely has time to recover himself again before another aspirant for his approval appears from dining room. It is* MRS. ORCUTT, *who has shed her workaday dress for something very grand in the way of a black silk dinner gown.*)

MRS. OR. (*Crossing* C. *to him—outstretched hands.*) David Kingsley! Little David Kingsley!
KINGS. (*A little bewildered, rises to meet the emergency.*) Why —how do you do! (*As he shakes hands.*)
MRS. OR. (*Coquettishly.*) Surely you remember me.
KINGS. (*Lying bravely.*) Of course I do.
MRS. OR. Who am I? (*He has an·instant of panic.*) Helen ——
KINGS. Helen ——
MRS. OR. Helen who?
KINGS. Helen ——
MRS. OR. Ro ——
KINGS. (*Catches desperately at this straw.*) Ro ——
MRS. OR. —mayne! Helen Romayne!
KINGS. (*Repeating it just the barest flash behind her.*) Helen Romayne. Why, of course! Well, what a charming surprise. Imagine your remembering me! A scrubby little kid in the office.
MRS. OR. But that little office boy became one of the most brilliant producers in the theatre. Those beautiful plays! I loved them all.
KINGS. So did I. But something happened to the theatre about that time. It was sort of shot from under us.
MRS. OR. But you've gone right on. You've risen to even greater triumphs in the pictures.
KINGS. (*Quietly ironic.*) Yes, even greater triumphs.

(*A step on the stair.* MRS. ORCUTT *turns.*)

MRS. OR. (*As she starts for dining room.*) Well—it was lovely see-ing you. I hope you'll be coming again.
KINGS. I hope so, too.

(MRS. ORCUTT *makes her escape as* JEAN *appears on stairs, re-splendent in her borrowed finery,* PAT'S *green taffeta, and* BOBBY'S *evening wrap.*)

27

JEAN. (*As she shakes hands.*) So glad to see you, Mr. Kingsley.

KINGS. I'm glad you managed to be free.

JEAN. I guess girls generally manage to be free when you invite them.

KINGS. You don't think maybe my being in the motion picture business has got something to do with it?

JEAN. Why, Mr. Kingsley, how can you say such a thing!

KINGS. You think it's all sheer charm, huh?

JEAN. Of course. . . . Look, would you mind awfully if I —— (*Calls upstairs.*) Terry! Come on!

TERRY. (*From above.*) I'm coming.

JEAN. That's Terry Randall, my roommate. Did you see " Cyclone "? Or " The Eldest Son "?

KINGS. Oh, yes. In " Cyclone " she was ——

JEAN. It was just a tiny part. She came into the drugstore.

KINGS. Oh, yes. Just a bit, but she was good. . . . Yes, she was excellent!

JEAN. Wasn't she?

(TERRY *comes down stairs.* TERRY *is still wearing the plain dark little dress in which we have previously seen her. If it were not for the glowing face she would seem rather drab in comparison to the dazzling* JEAN.)

TERRY. (*With great directness.*) Well, if you will come calling at a Girls' Club, Mr. Kingsley, what can you expect?

KINGS. I didn't expect anything as charming as this.

TERRY. Mm! You *are* in the moving picture business, aren't you?

KINGS. I am, Miss Randall. But my soul belongs to God.

JEAN. Don't you think she'd be good for pictures, Mr. Kingsley? Look. (*Turning* TERRY'S *profile to show to best advantage.*)

TERRY. I think I'd be terrible.

JEAN. Don't talk like that. Of course she's rehearsing now in the new Berger play. That is, she starts tomorrow.

KINGS. Good! I hear it's an interesting play.

TERRY. Do you know the first play I ever saw, Mr. Kingsley?

KINGS. No, what?

TERRY. It was your production of " Amaryllis."

KINGS. " Amaryllis! " You couldn't have seen that! That was my first production. Ten years ago.

TERRY. I did, though. I was eleven years old, and I saw it at

28

English's Opera House in Indianapolis. My mother took me. She cried all the way through it, and so did I. We had a lovely time.

KINGS. But " Amaryllis " wasn't a sad play.

TERRY. Oh, we didn't cry because we were sad. Mother cried because it brought back the days when she was an actress, and I cried because I was so happy. You see, we lived seventy-five miles from Indianapolis, and it was the first time I'd ever been in a theatre.

JEAN. Now, really, I don't think it's tactful to talk about the theatre to a picture man.

TERRY. I'm afraid I'm kind of dumb about pictures. Mother used to say the theatre had two offspring: the legitimate stage and the bastard.

JEAN. (*Taking* KINGSLEY *by the hand and pulling him from the room.*) Come on! And forget I ever introduced her to you.

(*He goes, calling, " Good-bye, Miss Randall."*)

TERRY. (*Calling after him.*) Oh, I hope I didn't ——

KINGS. (*As door closes on them.*) It's all right. I forgive you.

(*Left alone,* TERRY *suddenly realizes she has had no dinner. As she goes toward dining room she calls.*)

TERRY. Mattie! Mattie! (*Opens dining room doors.*) Oh, dear, is dinner over?

MATTIE. (*In dining room.*) Yes. I'm just clearing away.

TERRY. Oh, Mattie, darling, could you let me have just anything? Champagne and a little caviar?

MATTIE. (*In dining room.*) Well, I'll fix you a plate of something.

TERRY. You're an angel.

(*As* TERRY *turns away from dining room* KENDALL *is coming down stairs, dressed for the street. At sight of* TERRY *she pauses to chat.*)

KEN. Isn't it splendid, Terry, about your getting a job!

TERRY. It seems pretty dazzling to me, after six months. I only hope it's as big a hit as yours.

KEN. It's queer about being in a hit. You go through everything to get into one, and after a few months you're bored with it. It's like marriage. (*Doorbell rings—calls.*) It's all right, Mattie, I'll answer it. . . . Going out, Terry?

TERRY. Not tonight.

KEN. (*At street door.*) See you later.

(*A voice at the door: "Hello, there! Who are you?" KENDALL'S voice, a film of ice over it: "I beg your pardon!" The man's voice explains, "I'm looking for Jean Maitland." KENDALL calls, "Mattie!" and goes on her way. The call is unheard by MATTIE. KEITH BURGESS appears in archway. He is the kind of young man who never wears a hat. Turtle-necked sweater, probably black, unpressed tweed suit, unshaven.*)

KEITH. (*Comes in—to* C.) Where's Jean Maitland?

TERRY. (*Seated, chair* L. C.) In a taxi with a big moving picture man.

KEITH. She can't be. She had a date with me.

TERRY. Sorry. It isn't my fault.

KEITH. Who are you?

TERRY. Who wants to know?

KEITH. (D. C.) Are you an actress?

TERRY. Are you dizzy in the morning? Do you have spots before the eyes?

KEITH. My name is Keith Burgess.

TERRY. Is it?

KEITH. Don't you know who I am?

TERRY. Yes. You're a playwright, and you wrote a play called "Blood and Roses" that was produced at the Fourteenth Street Theatre, and it ran a week and it wasn't very good.

KEITH. It was the best goddam play that was ever produced in New York! And the one I'm writing now is even better.

TERRY. Mm! Maybe *two* weeks.

KEITH. (*Vastly superior.*) I don't think in terms of material success. Who cares whether a play makes money! All that matters is its message!

TERRY. But if nobody comes to see it who gets the message?

KEITH. I write about the worker! The masses! The individual doesn't count in modern society.

TERRY. But aren't the masses made up of individuals?

KEITH. Don't quibble!

TERRY. I'm so sorry.

30

(*Doorbell rings.*)

KEITH. I ask nothing as an individual. My work, my little room —that's all.

TERRY. No furniture?

(FRANK *crosses hall.*)

KEITH. A table, a chair, a bed. My books. My music.

(*The voice of* KAYE *at door.*)

KAYE. (*Off stage* R.) I'm Miss Hamilton, Kaye Hamilton.

(KEITH *moves* D. R.)

FRANK. Oh, yes, I think Mrs. Orcutt's expecting you.

(MRS. ORCUTT *appears in hallway from up* L., *just in time to greet the new arrival who enters up* R.)

MRS. OR. Glad to see you again, Miss Hamilton. Everything's in readiness for you. Frank, take Miss Hamilton's things right up. Oh! (*As she sees* TERRY *in living room.*) Terry, this is Kaye Hamilton, who's going to share the room with you and Jean. Terry Randall.

(TERRY *rises, goes* U. L. C.)

KAYE. I'll try not to be in the way.

TERRY. Oh, don't start that way! Grab your share of the closet-hooks.

KAYE. Thank you.

MRS. OR. (*As she shows* KAYE *upstairs.*) Now, if you'll just come with me I'll show you where everything is.

TERRY. (*As they start up.*) Let me know if I can be of any help.

MRS. OR. (*Talking as they ascend.*) If you have a trunk check Frank will take care of all that for you.

KAYE. No, no, I haven't got a trunk.

(*They are gone.* KEITH *throughout has been observing* TERRY *with an old-fashioned eye of appreciation.*)

KEITH. Hey! Turn around! (*She does so, rather wonderingly.*) You shouldn't wear your hair like that. It hides your face. (*Moves to L. C.*)

TERRY. (*Moves R. to couch.*) Oh, do you notice faces? I thought you were above all that.

KEITH. I notice everything. Your head's too big for the rest of you. You've got pretty legs, but you oughtn't to wear that kind of dress.

TERRY. (*Sits L. arm of couch.*) I suppose you're known as Beau Burgess! What the Well-Dressed Man Will Wear!

KEITH. Oh, you like snappy dressers, eh? Monograms and cuff-links.

TERRY. No, I don't meet very many monograms.

KEITH. (*Steps in. His gaze roaming around the room.*) What do you live in this place for? Do you like it?

TERRY. I love it. We live and breathe theatre, and that's what I'm crazy about.

KEITH. Are you? So am I. What do you want to do in the theatre? What kind of parts do you want to play?

TERRY. I want to play every kind of part I'm not suited for. Old hags of eighty and Topsy and Lady Macbeth. And what do I get? Ingenues—and very little of that.

KEITH. Don't take 'em. Wait till you get what you want.

TERRY. (*Rises. Moves D. R.*) Well, it's a nice idea. But did you ever hear of this thing called eating?

KEITH. (*Eases down after her.*) You mustn't think of that. Why, I've lived on bread and cocoa for days at a time. If you believe in something you've got to be willing to starve for it.

TERRY. (*Below couch.*) I am willing. But you don't know what it is to be an actress. If you feel something you can write it. But I can't act unless they let me. I can't just walk up and down my room, being an actress.

KEITH. It's just as tough for a writer. Suppose they won't produce his plays! I write about the iron-worker and they want Grand Dukes. I could write pot-boilers, but I don't. The theatre shouldn't be just a place to earn a living in. It should be thunder and lightning, and power and truth. (*Steps L.*)

TERRY. (*Eases L.*) And magic and romance!

KEITH. (*Turns R. to her.*) No, no! Romance is for babies! I write about *today!* I want to tear the heart out of the rotten carcass we call life and hold it up, bleeding, for all the world to see.

32

TERRY. (*Steps in to* KEITH.) How about putting some heart into life instead of tearing it out all the time?

KEITH. (*Eases* R.) There's no place for sentiment in the world today. We've gone past it.

TERRY. I suppose that's why you never hear of Romeo and Juliet.

KEITH. That's a woman's argument. (*Turns* L.)

TERRY. Well, I'm a woman.

KEITH. (*Eases* R.) Why haven't I run into you before? Where've you been all the time?

TERRY. I've been right here, in and out of every office on Broadway.

KEITH. Me, too. But I'm going to keep right on until they listen to me. And you've got to keep on, too.

TERRY. I will! I'm going to!

(MATTIE *appears in dining room door.*)

MATTIE. You-all want your dinner now, Miss Terry? It's ready.

TERRY. Oh, Mattie, I'd forgotten all about it.

KEITH. Never mind, Mattie. . . . How about dinner with me? We'll go to Smitty's and have a couple of hamburgers.

TERRY. With onions?

KEITH. Sure—onions! . . . (*Going.*) Say, what the hell's your name, anyhow?

(*Curtain cue. They go out* U. R. *The* TWO MARYS *come downstairs arguing about Clark Gable and Spencer Tracy as curtain falls.*)

## CURTAIN

## ACT I

SCENE 2: *One of the bedrooms. A pleasant enough but rather cramped room, with 3 beds, 3 dressers, 3 small chairs. There is a bathroom door down* L., *a window* C. *A door up* L. *leads to hall.*

*Each dresser reflects something of the personality and daily life of its owner. Stuck in the sides of the mirrors are snapshots, photographs, newspaper clippings, telegrams, theatre programs.*

*It is night, and through the window we get a glimpse
of the city's lights with electric sign through window one
quarter up.*

*At the beginning the room is unoccupied.*

KAYE *comes into the room from bathroom with towel
and comb, closes door. She is wearing a bathrobe over
her nightgown, goes to chair, puts towel over back, then
to window—pulls down shade—the electric sign blacks
out.* KAYE *goes to her dresser, which is conspicuously
bare of ornaments, souvenirs, or photographs. She opens
top drawer, takes out her handbag, removes her money
from a small purse and counts it, a process which
doesn't take long. Two dollars and sixty cents.*

*There is a knock at the door.*

KAYE. Yes?

JUDITH. (*As she opens door up* L.) Can I come in? Where's
Terry?

KAYE. She isn't back yet.

(JUDITH *is wearing sleeping pajamas and she is in the process of
doing her face up for the night. A net safeguards her curls.*)

JUD. (*As she crosses* R.) Look, do you think she'd mind if I borrowed some of her frowners? I forgot to get some.

KAYE. I think there's some in her top drawer.

JUD. (*As she pulls open drawer.*) Thanks. . . . You don't go out
much evenings, do you?

KAYE. (*As she puts lingerie on back of chair in bureau.*) No.

JUD. Any sign of a job yet?

KAYE. No, not yet.

JUD. Something'll turn up. It always does. (*She waits a moment
for* KAYE'S *answer, but there is none.*) You know, you're a funny
kid. You've been here a month, and I don't know any more about
you than when you came in. The rest of us are always spilling our
whole insides, but you never let out a peep. Nobody comes to see
you, no phone calls, never go out nights, you haven't even got a
picture on your dresser. Haven't you got any folks? Or a beau or
something? (*No sound from* KAYE. JUDITH *turns to glance at
her.*) Sorry. My mistake.

(*The voices of* BIG *and* LITTLE MARY *are heard in the hall.* BIG MARY: "*Mm, somebody's cooking something.*" LITTLE MARY: "*Smells like a rarebit.*" *The* TWO MARYS, *in hats and coats, stick their heads in at door.*)

LITTLE M. Who's cooking? You?
JUD. No—Madeleine. Where've you been? Show?
BIG M. We saw the Breadline Players in "Tunnel of Death."
LITTLE M. (*Dourly.*) Come on, let's get some rarebit before it's all gone.

(*They disappear down hallway.*)

JUD. (*Sits arm of chair* R.) Terry's late, isn't she? It's half-past eleven. And she isn't in the last act.
KAYE. She'll be here in a minute. Have you seen the play?
JUD. I haven't had time yet. I'm going tomorrow night.
KAYE. I didn't like it very much, but Terry's awfully good. Just a little part, but you always knew she was on.

(PAT *appears in doorway. She is wearing a tailored suit and hat.*)

PAT. (*Peering round.*) Anybody in here? . . . Well, off to the mines.
JUD. Oh, hello, Pat! Going to work?
PAT. Yes, the night shift. With a hey-nonny-nonny and a swiss on rye. (*Does a little floor-show dance step, and goes.*)
KAYE. I wonder what it's like working in a night club. I wish I'd learned to dance.
JUD. Well, with your looks you'll get along all right. (KAYE *is silent. By this time* JUDITH *has wandered over to* KAYE'S *dresser on other side of room up* L. *still continuing her beauty treatments.*) Where's your hand-mirror? Why, where's the whole set?
KAYE. I haven't got it any more.
JUD. (*A little too casually.*) It was—gold, wasn't it?
KAYE. Uh huh.
JUD. . . . Got any folks you have to support?
KAYE. (*Quietly.*) No, I haven't any folks.
JUD. (*To* JEAN'S *bureau up* R.; *starts creaming her hands.*) Well, if you want some, I'm the girlie that can fix you up. Five brothers and four sisters, and you couldn't scare up a dollar eighty among

the lot. I've got a little sister named Doris. Fifteen, and as innocent as Mata Hari. She's coming to New York next year to duplicate my success.

KAYE. (*Somewhat wistfully.*) I think it would be rather nice, having a little sister with you.

JUD. Yeh, only she won't be with me much. Two weeks and they'll have her in the Home for Delinquent Girls.

(TERRY *enters, a drooping figure. A glance at the two occupants of the room. Her back to door, she slowly closes it behind her and slumps against it.*)

KAYE. Hello!

JUD. Hello, Terry.

TERRY. Young lady, willing, talented, not very beautiful, finds herself at liberty. (*As she starts* R.) Will double in brass, will polish brass, will eat brass before very long. Hi, girls!

KAYE. Terry, what's the matter?

TERRY. We closed. Four performances and we closed.

KAYE. Terry, you didn't!

JUD. Tonight! But it's only Thursday!

TERRY. (*Sitting in chair* R.) Well, it seems you can close on Thursday just as well as Saturday—in fact, it's even better: it gives you two more days to be sunk in.

JUD. But it didn't get bad notices. What happened?

TERRY. We just got to the theatre tonight, and there it was on the call-board. "To the Members of the 'Blue Grotto' Company: You are hereby advised that the engagement of the 'Blue Grotto' will terminate after tonight's performance. Signed, Milton H. Schwepper, for Berger Productions, Incorporated."

KAYE. Terry, how ghastly!

JUD. Just like that, huh?

TERRY. Just like that. We stood there for a minute and read it. Then we sort of got together in the dressing rooms and talked about it in whispers, the way you do at a funeral. And then we all put on our make-up and gave the best damned performance we'd ever given.

JUD. Any other job in the world, if you get canned you can have a good cry in the washroom and go home. But show business! You take it on the chin and then paint up your face and out on the stage as gay as anything. "My dear Lady Barbara, what an enchanting place you have here! And what a quaint idea, giving us pig's knuckles for tea!"

TERRY. Yes, it was awfully jolly. I wouldn't have minded if Berger or somebody had come back stage and said, "Look, we're sorry to do this to you, and better luck next time." But nobody came around—not Berger, or the author, or the director or anybody. They can all run away at a time like that, but the actors have to stay and face it.

JUD. You'll get something else, Terry. You got swell notices in this one.

TERRY. Nobody remembers notices except the actors who get them.

KAYE. The movie scouts remember. What about your screen test?

JUD. Yes, how about that? Have you heard from it?

TERRY. (*Rises and up to bureau* R.) Oh, I'm not counting on that. They might take Jean. She's got that camera face. But they'll never burn up the Coast wires over me.

JUD. Jean can't act. You're ten times the actress that she is.

TERRY. (*Throwing herself across bed.*) Oh, how do you know who's an actress and who isn't! You're an actress if you're acting. Without a job and those lines to say, an actress is just an ordinary person, trying not to look as scared as she feels. What is there about it, anyhow? Why do we all keep trying?

BERN. (*Enters with mourning veil hat, followed by* MADELEINE *who has a dish in her hand.*) How do I look?

KAYE. Marvelous.

JUD. What are you?

BERN. I'm seeing the Theatre Guild tomorrow. They're going to revive "Madame X." (*Exit.*)

MAD. Anybody want some chop suey? Terry? Kaye?

TERRY. No, thank you.

KAYE. No, thanks.

JUD. (*Tempted by this.*) Chop suey? I thought it was rarebit.

MAD. We didn't have any beer, so I'm calling it chop suey. (*She goes.*)

JUD. Certainly sounds terrible. (*Crossing* L. *to door—turns with a hand on door.*) Look, I guess you want this closed, huh?

TERRY. Yes, please.

(*Door closes.* KAYE *and* TERRY *are alone. With a sigh* TERRY *again faces reality. Listlessly she begins to undress.* KAYE *is almost ready for bed. As she turns back bedclothes she pauses to regard* TERRY.'

37

KAYE. I know how sunk you feel, Terry. It's that horrible let-down after the shock has worn off.

TERRY. The idiotic part of it is that I didn't feel so terrible after the first minute. I thought, well, Keith's coming around after the show, and we'll go to Smitty's and sit there and talk and it won't seem so bad. But he never showed up.

KAYE. Terry, I shouldn't try to advise you where men are concerned. I haven't been very smart myself—but this isn't the first time he's let you down. Don't get in too deep with a boy like Keith Burgess. It'll only make you unhappy.

TERRY. I don't expect him to be like other people. I wouldn't want him to be. One of the things that makes him so much fun is that he's different. If he forgets an appointment it's because he's working and doesn't notice. Only I wish he had come tonight. (*She is pulling her dress over her head as she talks and her words are partly muffled until she emerges.*) I needed him so. (*Suddenly her defenses are down.*) Kaye, I'm frightened. For the first time, I'm frightened. It's three years now. The first year it didn't matter so much. I was so young. Nobody was ever as young as I was. I thought, they just don't know. But I'll get a good start and show them. I didn't mind anything in those days. Not having any money, or quite enough food; and a pair of silk stockings always a major investment. I didn't mind because I felt so sure that that wonderful part was going to come along. But it hasn't. And suppose it doesn't next year? Suppose it never comes?

KAYE. You can always go home. You've got a home to go to, anyhow.

TERRY. (*Rises.*) And marry some home-town boy—like Louise?

KAYE. I didn't mean that, exactly.

TERRY. I can't just go home and plump myself down on Dad. You know what a country doctor makes! When I was little I never knew how poor we were, because mother made everything seem so glamorous—so much fun. (*Starts L. for bathroom—all this time* TERRY *has continued her preparations for bed: hung up her dress, slipped her nightgown over her head.*) Even if I was sick it was a lot of fun, because then I was allowed to look at her scrap-book. I even used to pretend to be sick, just to look at it—and that took acting, with a doctor for a father. (*Exits and makes rest of change off stage continuing dialogue.*) I adored that scrap-book. All those rep-company actors in wooden attitudes—I remember a wonderful picture of mother as Esmeralda. It was the last part she ever played, and she never finished the performance.

KAYE. What happened?

TERRY. She fainted, right in the middle of the last act. They rang down and somebody said, " Is there a doctor in the house? " And there was. And he married her.

KAYE. Terry, how romantic!

TERRY. Only first she was sick for weeks and weeks. Of course the company had to leave her behind. They thought she'd catch up with them any week, but she never did.

KAYE. Didn't she ever miss it? I mean afterward.

TERRY. (*Coming back into room, crosses R. to bureau.*) I know now that she missed it every minute of her life. I think if Dad hadn't been such a gentle darling, and not so dependent on her, she might have gone off and taken me with her. I'd have been one of those children brought up in dressing rooms, sleeping in trunk trays, getting my vocabulary from stage-hands. (*As she creams her face.*)

KAYE. That would have been thrilling.

TERRY. But she didn't. She lived out the rest of her life right in that little town, but she was stage-struck to the end. There never was any doubt in her mind—I was going to be an actress. It was almost a spiritual thing, like being dedicated to the church.

KAYE. I never thought of the theatre that way. I just used it as a convenience, because I was desperate, and now I'm using it again because I'm desperate.

TERRY. Oh, now I've made you blue. I didn't mean to be gloomy. We're fine! We're elegant! They have to pay me two weeks' salary for this flop. Eighty dollars. We're fixed for two weeks. One of us'll get a job.

KAYE. I can't take any more money from you. You paid my twelve-fifty last week.

TERRY. Oh, don't be stuffy! I happened to be the one who was working.

KAYE. I'll never get a job. I'm—I'm not a very good actress.

TERRY. Oh, now!

KAYE. And there's nothing else I can do and nobody I can go back to. Except somebody I'll *never* go back to.

TERRY. It's your husband, isn't it?

KAYE. (*Looks at* TERRY *a moment, silently.*) I ran away from him twice before, but I had to go back. I was hungry, and finally I didn't even have a room. Both times, he just waited. He's waiting now.

TERRY. Kaye, tell me—what is it? Why are you afraid of him?

KAYE. (*Turns her eyes away from* TERRY *as she speaks.*) Because I know him. To most people he's a normal attractive man. But I know better. Nights of terror. "Now, darling, it wouldn't do any good to kill me. They wouldn't let you play polo tomorrow. Now, we'll open the window and you'll throw the revolver at that lamp-post. It'll be such fun to hear the glass smash." And then there were the times when he made love to me. I can't even tell you about that. (*She recalls the scene with a shudder.*)

TERRY. Kaye, darling! But if he's as horrible as that, can't you do something legally?

KAYE. (*A desperate shake of her head.*) They have millions. I'm nobody. I've gone to his family. They're united like a stone wall. They treated me as though I was the mad one.

TERRY. But, Kaye, isn't there anybody —— What about your own folks? Haven't you got any?

KAYE. I have a father. Chicago. I ran away at sixteen and went on the stage. Then I met Dick—and I fell for him. He was good-looking, and gay, and always doing sort of crazy things—smashing automobiles and shooting at bar-room mirrors. . . . I thought it was funny, *then.*

TERRY. And I've been moaning about my little troubles.

KAYE. You know, I'd sworn to myself I never was going to bother you with this. Now, what made me do it!

TERRY. I'm glad you did. It'll do you good.

KAYE. Yes, I suppose it will.

TERRY. (*As she takes counterpane off bed.*) Well, we might as well get those sheep over the fence. Maybe we'll wake up to-morrow morning and there'll be nineteen managers downstairs, all saying, "You and only you can play this part."

KAYE. I suppose Jean'll be out till all hours.

TERRY. (*At window, puts up shade—electric sign comes on one-quarter up.*) There's a girl who hasn't got any troubles. Life rolls right along for her. . . . (*Puts up window.*) Well, ready to go bye-bye?

KAYE. (*Switches off all lights except bed lamps—electric sign up to one-half.*) I suppose I might as well. But I feel so wide awake.

(*As* TERRY *opens window a blast of noise comes up from the* street. *A cacophony made up of protesting brakes, automobile horns, taxi drivers' shouts, a laugh or two.*)

1ST VOICE. (*Off.*) Hey, buddy, back her up a bit, will you?
2ND VOICE. (*Off.*) O. K., Bill.

(*From her dresser* KAYE *takes a black eyeshield and adjusts it over her eyes after she is in bed.* TERRY *does same, then shouts a Good night! loudly enough to be heard above the street din.* KAYE'S *Good night is equally loud. Simultaneously they turn out their bed lights. For a second—but only a second—the room is in darkness. Then the reason for* TERRY'S *eyeshade becomes apparent. A huge electric advertising sign on an adjacent roof flashes on, off, on, off, full up, alternately flooding the room with light and plunging it into darkness.*)

TERRY. (*Shouting.*) Funny if we both *did* get jobs tomorrow!
KAYE. Huh?
TERRY. (*Louder.*) I say, it would be funny if we both got jobs tomorrow!
KAYE. Certainly would.

(*A moment of silence. The door bursts open.* JEAN *comes in, bringing with her a quiver of excitement. She is in dinner clothes.*)

JEAN. (*Turns on light full up except bed lamps and bureau lamp. Electric sign dims one-half.*) Terry! Wake up!
TERRY. What's the matter?
JEAN. (*Slams window down—street noise stops.*) We're in the movies!
TERRY. What?
JEAN. Both of us! We're in the movies! They just heard from the Coast.
TERRY. Jean! How do you know? What happened?
JEAN. Mr. Kingsley just got the telegram. They liked the tests, and we're to go to the office tomorrow to sign our contracts. We leave for the Coast next week! Terry! Can you believe it!
KAYE. Oh, girls, how exciting!
TERRY. (*Bewildered.*) Yes. Yes. You mean—right away?
JEAN. Of course we'll only get little parts in the beginning. But there's that beautiful check every week, whether you work or not.

41

And the swimming and the sunshine and those little ermine jackets up to here. No more running around to offices and having them spit in your eye. And a salary raise every six months if they like us. So at the end of three years it begins to get pretty good, and after five years it's wonderful, and at the end of seven years it's more money than you ever heard of.

TERRY. Seven years! What do you mean—seven years!

JEAN. Yes, it's a seven-year contract—that is, if they take up the options.

TERRY. But what about the stage? Suppose I wanted to act?

JEAN. Well, what do you think this is—juggling? Motion picture acting is just as much of an art as stage acting, only it's cut up more. You only have to learn about a line at a time, and they just keep on taking it until you get it right.

TERRY. (*Staring at* JEAN. *A stricken pause. Then she shakes her head slowly. Her decision is made.*) Oh, no.

JEAN. What?

TERRY. I couldn't.

JEAN. Couldn't what?

TERRY. That isn't acting, that's piecework. You're not a human being, you're a thing in a vacuum. Noise shut out, human response shut out. But in the theatre, when you hear that lovely sound out there, then you know you're right. It's as though they'd turned on an electric current that hit you here. And that's how you learn to act.

JEAN. You can learn to act in pictures. You have to do it till it's right.

TERRY. Yes, and then they put it in a tin can, like Campbell's Soup. And if you die the next day it doesn't matter a bit. You don't even have to be alive to be in pictures.

JEAN. I suppose you call *this* being alive! Sleeping three in a room in this rotten dump. It builds you up, eh?

TERRY. I'm not going to stay here all my life. This is only the beginning.

JEAN. Don't kid yourself. You've been here three years, and then it's three years more, and then another three and where are you? You can't play ingenues forever. Pretty soon you're a character woman, and then you're running a boarding house like old Orcutt. *That'll* be nice, won't it?

TERRY. I don't know. You make me sound like a fool, but I know I'm not. All I know is I want to stay on the *stage*. I just don't

42

want to *be* in pictures. An actress in the theatre, that's what I've wanted to be my whole life. It isn't just a career, it's a feeling. The theatre is something that's gone on for hundreds and hundreds of years. It's—I don't know—it's part of civilization.

JEAN. All right, you stay here with your civilization, eating those stews and tapiocas they shove at us, toeing the mark in this female seminary, buying your clothes at Klein's. That's what you like, eh?

TERRY. *Yes*, I like it!

JEAN. And I suppose you like this insane racket going on all night! (*She throws open window—street noises start.*)

TERRY. (*Yelling above noise.*) Yes, I do!

JEAN. And that Cadillac car sign going on and off like a damned lighthouse! (*She turns off light. Again we see the flash of electric sign, off, on, off, on, full up and flashing faster.*) I suppose you've got to have that to be an actress!

TERRY. Yes! Yes! Yes! Yes! Yes!

JEAN. (*Not stopping for her.*) Well, not for me. I'm going out where there's sunshine and money and fun and ——

TERRY. (*Shouting above her.*) And little ermine swimming pools up to here!

(*The street noise, the flashing light, and their angry shouts are still going on as curtain descends.*)

JEAN. (*As curtain falls.*) I'm going to make something out of my life. I'm not going to stay in this lousy dump.

## CURTAIN

# ACT II

SCENE 1: *Same as Act I, Scene 1. Mid-morning, sunlight is streaming in.*

FRANK *is rather listlessly pushing a carpet-sweeper, his attention directed toward an open newspaper lying on a chair. He edges nearer and nearer, his movements with the sweeper become slower and slower, until finally they are barely perceptible.*

ANN *comes briskly downstairs with a condescending " Good morning, Frank!" and goes into dining room,* FRANK'S *response having been an absent-minded mumble.* MATTIE *bustles in from dining room, and her face reflects her irritation as she sees* FRANK'S *idling at this busy hour. Lips compressed, she marches straight to him, snatches sweeper from him and goes off with it.* FRANK *follows meekly after.*

*Somewhere in the hall, unseen, a clock strikes eleven.*

BOBBY, *gaily singing, skips downstairs and stops for a look through the mail. She finds a letter that gets her full attention, so that she is absorbed in it as she walks more slowly toward dining room. After dropping her coat and hat on table back of couch* R.

JUDITH *enters* L. *with coat over arm.*

JUD. Hello, Bobby!

BOBBY. Oh, say! Here's a letter from Madeleine.

JUD. Where is she this week?

BOBBY. Let's see. This week, Portland and Spokane. Next week, Seattle. (*Exits dining room.*)

JUD. Seattle. That's her home town. (KENDALL *dashes downstairs, struggling into one coat sleeve as she comes.*) Heh, where're you going?

KEN. Rehearsal!

JUD. What's the rush?

KEN. Late! (*Exits up* R.)

JUD. (*Calling after her as she dashes for door.*) You're too conscientious. (*Door slams.*) Never gets you anywhere in this business.

TERRY. (*Coming downstairs.*) Well, what *does* get you anywhere, if I may make so bold?

JUD. Clean living, high thinking, and an occasional dinner with the manager.

TERRY. (*Taking a look through mail.*) What time is it? Shouldn't you be at rehearsal?

JUD. (*Drops coat and hat on armchair* L.) No, there's plenty of time. The nuns aren't called until eleven-thirty today.

TERRY. (*Turning over envelope in her hand.*) Mrs. Robert Hendershot—why, that's Louise! Appleton, Wisconsin. It's a letter from Louise.

(*Phone rings.* TERRY *rips open envelope and takes a quick look at its pages, which are voluminous.*)

JUD. (*En route to phone.*) Maybe it's a Little Stranger. She's been married a year. . . . Hello! . . . She's right here. . . . (*Hands phone to* TERRY.) The boy friend.

TERRY. Keith? (*Thrusts letter into* JUDITH'S *hand, who drops down* R. *to couch and sits.*) Read—it's addressed to all of us. (*As* JUDITH *buries herself in letter* TERRY'S *attention goes to phone.*) Keith! Isn't this the middle of the night for you! . . . What about? . . . No, I've got to stay free all afternoon on account of Dad. . . . Yes, he's driving all the way from Elvira. Well, you don't *have* to like it. *He* will. . . . No, I can't, because he's only here a day and a half, and this afternoon he wants to see Radio City and the Medical Center and the Battery.

JUD. (*Looking up from letter.*) Has he got a bicycle?

TERRY. And don't forget that you've invited us to dinner. . . . No, not at Smitty's. . . . Well, Dad and Smitty's just don't *go* together. And look, darling, don't wear a black shirt and don't be one of the Masses tonight. . . . What? . . . Well, you can tell me about it at dinner. . . . No, I can't, I've got a radio rehearsal.

JUD. (*Still with letter.*) Say, this is a classic.

TERRY. Well, if it's as vital as all that you can come up here. . . . That's my brave boy! (*She bangs up.*)

JUD. (*Her first opportunity to read from letter.*) Get this. " I have gained a little weight, but Bob says I look better not so scrawny. He says maybe I like my own cooking too much, but then he is always joking."

TERRY. (*To* OLGA, *who enters* L. *Crossing to* C.) It's a letter from Louise. (*As she sits on couch* R.)

OLGA. What does she say?

BOBBY. (*Appearing in dining room doorway.*) Who said a letter from Louise?

TERRY. Yes, it just came.

JUD. (*Reading as* ANN *and* SUSAN *come into dining room doorway to hear the news.*) "Dear Girlies: I guess you all wonder why I have not written for so long. I honestly don't know where the year has gone to. First there was the house to furnish. We've got the darlingest six-room bungalow on Winnebago Street. And then of course everybody was giving parties for me, and after that I had to return the obligation by giving parties for them. We are all even now. I gave the last one just yesterday—eighteen girls of the young married set, three tables of bridge and one of mah jong, and two people just talked. The luncheon was lovely, if I do say so. Everything pink."

OLGA. You're making it up.

JUD. So help me. . . . "I am a member of the Ladies' Committee at the Country Club, which gives wonderful Saturday night dances during the summer." (*To the girls.*) Japanese lanterns. . . . "But do not think that I have lost track of the theatre. We take the *Milwaukee Sentinel* daily and last week we drove to Milwaukee and saw Walter Hampden in 'Cyrano.'"

TERRY. (*Reaching for letter.*) Let me see! "So now I've told you all my news and you've got to write me just everything about the Club. What about you, Terry, have you got a swell part for this season? I thought I'd die when I saw Jean's picture in *Photoplay* all dressed up like a real movie star in a little ermine jacket and everything. Jean a movie star! I've been bragging to all my friends. Well, if you girls think about me as much as I do about you, my ears would be about burned off. We have supper here around six o'clock, just as you all do at the Club, and when it's over I always think, well, the girls are all beating it down to the show-shop and making up to go on and just knocking the audience cold. Only I don't say it out loud any more because Bob says, Oh, for God's sake, you and your club! Love to old Orcutt and for goodness' sakes, write, write, WRITE!"

46

JUD. (*Very low.*) Wow.

TERRY. (*Rising.*) Well, I'll never complain again. This makes my eighteen a week on the radio look pretty wonderful.

OLGA. (*As she goes upstairs.*) Everything pink.

BOBBY. We've just been livin' in a bed of roses.

ANN. I could have told her when she left it wouldn't work.

(BOBBY, ANN *and* SUSAN *go back to dining room.* TERRY *and* JUDITH *remain.*)

JUD. (*Getting into her coat.*) Well, I might as well get down to the factory.

TERRY. Look, Judith. Think you'll be rehearsing all afternoon?

JUD. How do I know! This thing I'm in is a combination of Ringling Brothers and the Passion Play. You never know whether they're going to rehearse us nuns or the elephants.

TERRY. (*Sitting on couch.*) It's just that I'd love you to meet my father, if you have time.

JUD. Oh, I want to. He sounds like a cutie.

TERRY. I wonder what's on Keith's mind, getting up so early?

JUD. Nothing, is my guess.

TERRY. Judith! Maybe he sold the play!

JUD. Maybe. (*Takes plunge.*) Look, Terry. Where're you heading in with that guy, anyhow?

TERRY. Why, what do you mean?

JUD. *You* know. He's been coming around here for a year, taking all your time, talking about himself, never considering you for a minute. Sold his play! Well, if he has he can thank *you* for it. It's as much your play as his.

TERRY. That isn't true.

JUD. Don't tell *me*. It was nothing but a stump speech the way he wrote it. You made him put flesh and blood into it.

TERRY. (*Quietly.*) You're talking about someone you don't understand.

JUD. O. K. Forget I ever brought it up. . . . Well—good-bye. (*Starting off.*)

TERRY. (*Rather reserved.*) Good-bye. (*Takes 2 typewritten pages out of her handbag.*)

JUD. (*Stops, drops down to back of couch.*) Oh, now you're sore at me. I never can learn to keep my trap shut. But I only said it because I think more of you than anybody else in this whole menagerie. . . . Forgiven?

TERRY. Of course, Judy darling.

JUD. (*Indicating papers in* TERRY'S *hand.*) What's that? Your radio?

TERRY. Mm.

JUD. It makes me boil to think of an actress like you reading radio recipes for a living. (*Peers at script.*) "Two eggs and fold in the beaten whites." The beaten whites! That's us!

TERRY. (*As she rises and crosses* L.) Anyhow, it's a living for a few weeks. Aunt Miranda's Cooking Class.

JUD. Well, you're a hell of an Aunt Miranda, that's all I can say. . . . (*Goes out door up* R.)

(ANN *and* BOBBY *come out of dining room.* ANN *is carrying newspaper.* BOBBY *crosses* R. *to table, puts on coat.*)

ANN. (*Seeing* TERRY.) Did you read about Jean out in Hollywood?

TERRY. No. Where?

ANN. They've given her a new contract with a big raise and she's going to play the lead in " Two for Tonight."

TERRY. Really! (*Looking over* ANN'S *shoulder.*) How marvelous! (*Takes paper from* ANN *and goes into dining room.*)

BOBBY. It's all a matter of cheekbones. You've got to have a face like this. (*She pushes her round little face into hollow curves.*)

ANN. (*Gets her coat from piano.*) Are you going out job-hunting this morning?

BOBBY. Uh huh.

ANN. Where are you going?

BOBBY. Ah thought Ah'd go round to Equity and see what's up on the bulletin-board. Maybe there's something new casting.

ANN. (*Applying lipstick.*) I'm going to try a couple of agents' offices. (*Becomes unintelligible as she paints the cupid's bow.*) Sometimes they know about new things.

BOBBY. What kind of lipstick's that?

ANN. It's a new one. It's called " I'll Never Tell."

BOBBY. Let me see. (*Tries a daub on back of her hand.*) Mm. It's too orangey for me. Ah like Hibiscus—good and red—as if you'd been kicked in the mouth by a mule.

(*They gather up their handbags and go.* KAYE *comes downstairs like a little wraith. Near the foot of stairs she glances over railing and it is evident that she is relieved to find the room empty. As she is about to go to street door* MRS. ORCUTT *swoops down on her up* L. *with a promptness which indicates that she has been waiting for her.)*

MRS. OR. Oh, Kaye! Could I speak to you just a minute, please?

KAYE. I'm—just on my way to rehearsal.

MRS. OR. (*Crossing to dining room* L. *As she carefully closes dining room doors.*) I won't detain you but a second. I just want to —— (*The door is closed. As she comes back* L. C.) You must know how reluctant I always am to speak to you on this subject. I try to be as easy as I can with the girls but, after all, I have my bills to pay, too.

KAYE. But, Mrs. Orcutt, I'm rehearsing. You know that. And just the minute we open I can start paying off.

MRS. OR. Yes, I know. But plays are not always successful, and the amount has grown rather large. So, taking everything into consideration, I wonder if you'd mind a little suggestion.

KAYE. No. No.

MRS. OR. Well, it occurred to me that perhaps it might be wise if you were to find some place a little cheaper. By a lucky chance I think I know the ideal place. Of course the girls are a little older, and it's not strictly a theatrical club—more the commercial professions. However, I think you'll find it almost as conveniently situated. Forty-ninth Street, this side of Tenth Avenue. Perhaps, when you have time, you might drop in and look at it. (KAYE *only nods a silent assent.*) Now, now, we mustn't be upset by this. It's just a little talk. (*A rather grim pause which suggests the alternative.*)—Now, let's put it out of our minds. Shall we? And let me see a little smile. (*As there is no response from* KAYE, MRS. ORCUTT *smiles for both.*) There!—Well, we both have our day's work to do. (MRS. ORCUTT *goes up* L.)

(PAT, *singing blithely, comes down stairs. As she passes* KAYE U. C. *she chucks her gaily under the chin, says, "H'ya, Baby?" by way of morning greeting, and executes a brief and intricate little dance step, all this without pausing on her way to dining room.* KAYE *stands, a little wooden figure. Turns to go as* TERRY *comes in from dining room.)*

49

TERRY. What are you doing—going without your breakfast? (*Going upstairs.*)

KAYE. I don't want any breakfast. I'm not hungry.

TERRY. (*On her way upstairs.*) Well, you're just an old fool, rehearsing on an empty stomach.

(*As* KAYE *goes the* TWO MARYS *come into sight on stairs, talking as they descend. They pass* TERRY *as she goes up*)

BIG M. (*In the throes of trying to memorize a part.* LITTLE MARY, *who is cueing her, follows with the part in her hand.*) "Three weeks now since he first came here. What do we know about him —uh—anyhow?" Is there an "anyhow"?

LITTLE M. Yeh.

BIG M. "What do we know about him anyhow?"

LITTLE M. "I tell you ——"

(*Doorbell rings.*)

BIG M. "I tell you there is something mysterious going on in this house." Well, that's all, give me the cue.

LITTLE M. (*Scans part.*) Uh—huh ——

BIG M. Oh, for heaven's sake! "We must call the police."

LITTLE M. Oh, yeh. "We must call the police."

(MATTIE *crosses through hallway to answer bell.*)

BIG M. Now let's go back and do it right. "I tell you there is something mysterious going on in this house."

LITTLE M. (*As they go into dining room.*) "We must call the police."

(*Outer door is opened and we hear a voice subsequently identified as that of* MRS. SHAW, LINDA'S *mother.*)

MRS. SHAW. Good morning.

MATTIE. How-do.

MRS. S. This is the Footlights Club, isn't it?

MATTIE. Yes, ma'am. Won't you come in?

MRS. S. Oh, thank you. (MRS. SHAW *comes into sight. She is rather cosy little woman of about 55, plainly dressed, sweet-faced and*

*inclined to be voluble. She speaks rather confidently now to* MAT-
TIE.) I'm Mrs. Shaw, Linda's mother. She doesn't know I'm coming. I'm surprising her.

MATTIE. Oh—you Miss Linda's mother! For land's sakes!

MRS. S. She doesn't know I'm here. We live in Buffalo. I just got
off the train and came right up. Linda hasn't gone out, I hope?

MATTIE. (*As she goes toward stairs.*) No, I haven't seen her
around yet.

MRS. S. Well, you just tell her there's somebody here to see her,
very important. Only don't tell her it's her mother.

MATTIE. Yes'm. (*She disappears.*)

(MRS. SHAW *sits on couch and looks about her with bright-eyed
interest.* SUSAN *comes out of dining room, and nods politely.*)

MRS. S. Good morning.

SUSAN. Good morning.

MRS. S. Are you a little actress?

SUSAN. Yes, sort of.

MRS S. I'm Linda's mother. I've come to surprise her.

SUSAN. Oh, what fun!

MRS. S. Which one of the girls are you? Perhaps Linda's written
me about you.

SUSAN. I'm Susan Paige.

MRS. S. Are you acting a part on Broadway?

SUSAN. I'm in "Petticoat Lane," but I'm only an understudy.

MRS. S. Understudy?

SUSAN. That means I play the part in case the leading woman
gets sick.

MRS. S. Oh! That's nice. And does she get sick often?

SUSAN. Never! (SUSAN *goes upstairs as* MATTIE *descends.*)

(MATTIE *appears slightly flustered.*)

MATTIE. I'm awful sorry, I must have made a mistake. I guess
Miss Linda must have gone out already.

MRS. S. (*Rising.*) Oh, dear! Does anybody know where she went?

MATTIE. (*Edging toward dining room.*) Well, I'll see—maybe
Mrs. Orcutt knows. (*We have not heard the front door open or
close, so silently has* LINDA *entered the house. She is swiftly tiptoeing upstairs as* MATTIE *turns and sees her.*) There she is! Miss

Linda! Miss Linda! (LINDA *has not heeded the first call, but the second one stops her.*) Your ma's here.

MRS. S. Oh, dear, I was going to surprise you.

LINDA. (*Frozen on stairs.*) Why—mother!

MRS. S. I guess I have. Well, aren't you going to come down? (*Holds her arms open wide to embrace her.*)

(LINDA *makes a slow and heavy-footed descent, eyeing first her mother, then* MATTIE. *She is wrapped in a camel's-hair ulster, a little too large for her.*)

LINDA. (*Coming downstairs.*) Mother, how—how wonderful. When did—you ——

MRS. S. Why, Linda, child, aren't you glad to see me?

LINDA. Of course I am, mother. (*Kisses mother quickly and backs away.*)

MRS. S. (*As she surveys* LINDA'S *strange attire.*) Well, of all the funny get-ups!

LINDA. Yes, isn't it silly—I —— (*She turns to the gaping* MATTIE.) Mattie, I'm sure you have your work to do. Why don't you run along?

MATTIE. (*Reluctant to leave.*) Yes—Miss Linda. (*She goes.*)

MRS. S. Where did you get that coat? I never saw that coat before.

LINDA. It belongs to—to one of the girls. I had to go down to the drug store.

MRS. S. Why—you've got on evening slippers!

LINDA. I just put on the first thing I could find.

MRS. S. Linda Shaw, if you've run out in your pajamas —— (*Goes to* LINDA *as though to open the coat.*)

LINDA. (*Backing away from her mother.*) No, I haven't. I —— (*She realizes she has made a blunder.*) Yes, I have. Yes.

MRS. S. Linda, what are you wearing under that coat? (LINDA *stands, holding coat about her.*) Take off that coat! Take off that —— (*She jerks it open so that it slides down the girl's arms and drops to floor, revealing* LINDA *in a black satin evening dress of extreme cut—the narrowest of shoulder-straps, bare shoulders, a deep decolletage, the bodice almost backless.*) Linda!

LINDA. I spent the night with a girl friend.

MRS. S. Oh—Linda!

LINDA. Oh, mother, don't make a scene!

MRS. S. (*With repressed emotion.*) Linda, go up and pack your things. You're coming home with me.

LINDA. Oh, no, I'm not.

MRS. S. Linda Shaw!

LINDA. We can't talk here, mother. And there's no use talking, anyhow. I'm never coming home. I'm twenty-two years old, and my life is my own.

MRS. S. Who—who is this man? Are you going to marry him?

LINDA. He *is* married.

MRS. S. I'm going to send for your father. He'll know what to do.

LINDA. Mother, if you make a fuss about this I'll have to leave the club. That girl knows already. And if I leave here I'll go live with him, and the whole world will know it. Now take your choice.

(MRS. ORCUTT *enters from dining room, apprehension in her face, steeled for any eventuality. Her quick eye goes from the girl to the mother.*)

MRS. OR. I'm Mrs. Orcutt, Mrs. Shaw. My maid just told me you were here.

MRS. S. Oh, how do you do, Mrs. Orcutt?

MRS. OR. I understand you arrived unexpectedly.

MRS. S. Yes, I came down to do a bit of shopping and surprise my little girl here, and we practically came in together. She spent the night with my niece and her husband—86th Street—they had a rather late party and Linda just decided to —— I don't see how these young people stand it. . . . (*A little laugh.*) Doesn't she look silly—this time of day? Linda darling, do run up and change. Why don't you meet me for luncheon at the hotel? Can you do that?

LINDA. Of course, mother dear.

MRS. S. I'm at the Roosevelt, darling. Shall we say one o'clock?

LINDA. (*In quiet triumph.*) Yes, mother darling. (*She goes upstairs.*)

MRS. S. Oh, well, I must run along. I'm only going to be here a day or two and—well, good-bye.

MRS. OR. (*Accompanying her to door.*) Good-bye. It's been *so* nice. I'm always happy to meet the parents of our girls. And I hope that whenever you are in the city again you won't fail to drop in on us. Well, good-bye.

(*As* MRS. ORCUTT *passes back along hallway* OLGA *descends stairs. She is wearing a hat, her coat is over her arm. In one hand she has a few sheets of music, in the other a music portfolio. She tosses her coat over piano. She sits at piano, plays a few bars of music.* BERNICE, *in hat and coat, comes downstairs. She looks in on* OLGA *and listens to music, which is the second part of Rachmaninoff's Prelude in G Minor.*)

BERN. Are you going to play that at your concert?
OLGA. (*Playing.*) Yes.
BERN. When's it going to be?
OLGA. In the spring.
BERN. Whereabouts, Town Hall?
OLGA. Yes, yes.
BERN. Are you going to play under your own name?
OLGA. (*Stops playing and turns.*) Certainly.
BERN. Well, you've got an interesting name—Olga Brandt. It sounds like a musician. But Bernice Niemeyer! I think that's what's holding me back in the theatre. (OLGA *continues to play.*) Do you know what? I thought maybe I'd take one of those one-word names, the way some actresses do. I thought, instead of Bernice Niemeyer, I'd just call myself—Zara. (BERNICE *goes.*)

(OLGA *continues with her music. Chopin B Minor Etude, Op. 25, No. 10. Doorbell rings.* MATTIE *answers. As door opens we hear the voice of* DR. RANDALL, TERRY'S *father. His first words are lost under cover of* OLGA'S *music.*)

MATTIE. Just go right in and sit down. I'll tell Miss Terry you're here. (*She goes upstairs.*)

(DR. RANDALL *is a gentle-looking, gray-haired man touching 60. There is about him a vague quality—a wistful charm—that is not of the modern professional world.* OLGA, *as he enters, is about to launch herself on the finale of the selection she has been playing. It entails terrific chords, discords, and actual physical effort. The length of the keyboard seems scarcely adequate.* DR. RANDALL *stands arrested by this. Three times the music pauses as if finished, each time* DR. RANDALL *steps forward to speak, and* OLGA *starts again. He gives a little nod of approval as* OLGA *finishes, rises, and gathers up her music and her coat.* OLGA *acknowledges this with a*

54

*little inclination of her head, and goes. The front door slams on her going. Immediately the dining room doors open and the TWO MARYS come out, still deep in rehearsal, and start upstairs.)*

BIG M. " I tell you there is something mysterious going on in this house."
LITTLE M. " We must call the police."
BIG M. *(With no particular expression.)* " Last night I heard moans and shrieks, and this morning a dead man was found on the doorstep, his head completely severed."
LITTLE M. " What about the blood in the library? "

*(Both exit upstairs. PAT emerges from dining room, intent on mastering a fast and intricate dance routine for which she provides her own music. She, too, goes toward hall and upstairs. DR. RANDALL has barely had time to react to these somewhat bewildering encounters when a gay high voice from stairs calls, " Dad!" and TERRY comes running down. She hurls herself into her father's arms.)*

DR. RANDALL. Terry!
TERRY. Dad! Darling! I couldn't be more surprised.
DR. R. Glad to see me?
TERRY. Glad! I should say so! It's been almost a year.
DR. R. Too long, my dear. Too long to be separated. . . . Let me look at you.
TERRY. Bursting with health, Doc.
DR. R. Mmmmm. *(Pulls down first one eyelid, then other.)* Look kind of peaked to me. Eat enough greens?
TERRY. Greens! I'm a regular Miss Popeye. Now let me look at you. Say Ah, say Oo, say you love me. *(He laughs as he kisses her.)* Now come on and tell me everything. *(As she takes his coat and hat.)* How's Aunt Lucy? And is she taking good care of you!
DR. R. *(Goes to couch, sits.)* Say, you know Lucy! You'd think I was ten years old.
TERRY. *(Sitting on couch.)* I know. Wear your rubbers, have you got a clean handkerchief. Didn't she fuss about your driving all this way?
DR. R. Carried on like mad.
TERRY. How did you get here so early? You said afternoon. What happened?

DR. R. Well, when Stacy invited me to come East with him, I didn't know what kind of driver he was. Turned out he's one of those fellows slows down to eighty going through a town. I dozed off a couple of minutes, once, and missed all of Pennsylvania.

TERRY. He shouldn't have done it, but it *does* give me more time with you.

DR. R. Now maybe you've got things to do. You weren't expecting me till three or four.

TERRY. I've got nothing but a silly radio rehearsal. You know— I'm the big butter-and-egg girl. I'll be all through by quarter past one. Let's have lunch way up on top of something. Shall we?

DR. R. (*As he takes envelope from pocket.*) That's fine. Gives me time to drop in at the Polyclinic a few minutes. 345 West 50th Street. Where's that?

TERRY. It's not five minutes from here. And I'll pick you up at your hotel. Where are you?

DR. R. New Yorker. Stacy's idea. Full of go-getters.

TERRY. After lunch we'll whirl all over town. We'll see everything. Tonight we're going to the theatre, and Keith's taking us to dinner.

DR. R. Oh, yes. Your young man. I want to meet the boy.

TERRY. Now, Dad, remember, he's not like the boys back in Elvira.

DR. R. Say, *they're* not like that any more, either.

TERRY. Yes, but Keith's not like anybody you ever met. He's brilliant, and he's written the most marvelous play, and he hates the government and won't wear evening clothes.

DR. R. Sounds as if he didn't have a nickel.

TERRY. Oh, but he will have! This play will put him over. It's thrilling and beautiful! And oh, Dad, I'm going to play the leading part.

DR. R. Why, Tress, that's wonderful. Your mother would have been very proud.

TERRY. Of course he hasn't sold the play yet. But he will. He's bound to.

DR. R. Say, I'm going to come back and see you in it, if it takes my last nickel.

TERRY. (*Who has been eyeing him a little anxiously.*) Dad.

DR. R. Yes, Tress?

TERRY. You look as though you'd been working too hard. Have you?

DR. R. I wish I could say I had. But the fact is my waiting room looks pretty bleak these days.

TERRY. Isn't anybody sick at all? How about old Mrs. Wainwright?

DR. R. Yes, folks get sick, all right.

TERRY. Well, then!

DR. R. Well, it seems just being a medical man isn't enough, these days. If you had a cold, we used to just cure the cold. But nowadays, the question is, why did you *get* the cold? Turns out it's because, subconsciously, you didn't want to live. And why didn't you want to live? Because when you were three years old the cat died, and they buried it in the back yard without telling you, and you were in love with the cat, so, naturally, forty years later, you catch cold.

TERRY. But who tells them all this?

DR. R. Why—uh—young fellow came to town a few months ago; opened up offices.

TERRY. Oh!

DR. R. Sun lamps, X-ray machines, office fixed up like a power plant. He's the one's looking after Mrs. Wainwright. She's bedridden with sciatica, arthritis and a heart condition, but fortunately it's all psychic.

TERRY. Dad, do you mean he's taken away your whole practice from you!

DR. R. Mm—not as bad as that. The factory folks still come to me.

TERRY. But they haven't any money!

DR. R. They still have babies.

TERRY. Never you mind. I'm going to buy you the biggest, shiniest sun-lamp machine ever invented; and fluoroscopes and microscopes and stethoscopes and telescopes. You'll be able to sit in your office and turn a button and look right *through* Mrs. Wainwright, six blocks away.

DR. R. How about that new doctor? Will it go through him?

TERRY. It'll *dissolve* him.

(KEITH *strides to front of stairs. The black sweater has given way to a black shirt. Otherwise his costume is about the same. No hat, of course.*)

KEITH. (*Shouts upstairs.*) Terry!

TERRY. Oh—Keith!

KEITH. (*Dropping down* C.) Oh! I —— The door was open. I came right in.

TERRY. Here's father! He got here this morning.

KEITH. (*Advancing, shakes hands.*) Well! This is indeed a pleasure, sir.

DR. R. Thank you, young man. I'm glad to know you.

KEITH. Terry has told me so much about you. I've been looking forward to this meeting for a long time.

DR. R. Oh, that's very good of you.

KEITH. (*Takes out a crumpled pack of Camels.*) May I offer you a cigarette, sir?

DR. R. Thank you. (*Takes cigarette.*)

TERRY. (*Who has been observing all this courtliness with a growing bewilderment.*) Keith, what are you up to?

KEITH. You never told me, Theresa, that you and your father had such a strong resemblance. The same fine brow, the deep-set, ·thoughtful eyes. Allow me, sir! (*Lights* DR. RANDALL'S *cigarette.*)

TERRY. Keith, will you stop it! What is this act, anyhow?

KEITH. (*Blandly.*) It's no act. What are you talking about?

DR. R. (*Pats* KEITH *on shoulder.*) I guess you'll do. . . . Well, children, I've got to be off. You said quarter past one, Terry?

TERRY. (*As she gets his coat and hat.*) Yes, father. I'll pick you up at your hotel.

DR. R. (*To* KEITH.) Understand we're seeing you later. That right?

KEITH. (*Absent-mindedly crossing* L.) What? Oh. Yes.

TERRY. (*As she accompanies her father into hallway, their arms about each other's shoulders.*) I can't tell you how grand it is to have you here, Dad. . . . Now, don't cross against the lights, and promise to take taxis. Don't try to find places by yourself.

DR. R. All right, all right.

TERRY. I'll be at the hotel at one-fifteen.

DR. R. I'll be waiting.

TERRY. Good-bye, darling.

DR. R. Good-bye.

(TERRY *returns to living room and* KEITH.)

TERRY. Really, Keith, you can be so maddening. What was all that " Yes, sir," and " How are you, sir "?

KEITH. Can't I be polite?

TERRY. One of the least convincing performances I ever saw.

KEITH. That's right. Hit a fellow when he's down.

TERRY. Keith, what's the matter?

58

KEITH. I come to you in one of the toughest spots I ever was in in my life, and you jump all over me.

TERRY. I'm so sorry. I didn't know. How could I—what's happened? Is it the play?

KEITH. (*Unhappily.*) Yes.

TERRY. They all turned it down?

KEITH. (*Reluctantly.*) N-no.

TERRY. Keith! Tell me!

KEITH. (*Unwillingly.*) I—I could sign a contract this afternoon.

TERRY. You don't mean it! Who with?

KEITH. Gilman.

TERRY. (*Almost with awe.*) Gilman! Why, he's the best there is!

KEITH. (*Crossing R. to couch.*) That's what makes it so tough.

TERRY. (*After him.*) Keith, for heaven's sake, you're not being unreasonable about this! A Gilman production—why, it's —— Keith, no matter what he wants you to do, you've got to do it What's he want you to change? The second act?

KEITH. No. He likes the play all right. He's nuts about it.

TERRY. Well, then I don't—understand what ——

KEITH. (*Squirming.*) I just can't let him have it, that's all.

TERRY. (*Something clicks in her mind.*) Keith! It's *me.* He doesn't want *me.*

KEITH. Well—you see—Gilman's got Natalie Blake under contract, and she *is* a big star, and it just happens to be the kind of part she's been looking for ——

TERRY. (*Crushed.*) Did you tell him you thought I would be good in it?

KEITH. Of course. I gave him a hell of an argument. But he just won't do it unless Blake is in it.

TERRY. (*Turns, moves L. C.*) Well, then, that's—that. I wouldn't do anything to —— I bow out, Keith.

KEITH. (*After her.*) Gosh, Terry! You mean you really would do that for me!

TERRY. The play is the important thing, Keith. I love every single line of it. You didn't think, after the way we've worked on it for a whole year, that I was going to stand in the way, did you?

KEITH. God, you're wonderful, Terry! You're a great kid! I'm crazy about you! (*He tries to embrace her.*)

TERRY. (*Evading him.*) Please, Keith.

KEITH. There isn't one girl in a million would have taken it like that. And I love you for it. Love you, do you hear!

TERRY. Yes, Keith.

KEITH. I knew I could count on you to ——

(LINDA *comes down stairs, dressed for the street, carrying a small and costly looking dressing-case. Her manner is that of a determined and scornful girl.*)

LINDA. (*Pauses as she sees* TERRY. *A swift glance down hall. She decides to use* TERRY *as her messenger.*) Terry. Terry, will you do something for me?

TERRY. (*Absorbed in her own thoughts.*) What? Oh, hello, Linda.

LINDA. I don't want to see Orcutt. Will you give her a message for me?

TERRY. Yes, of course.

LINDA. Tell her I'm leaving. I'll send for my things this afternoon. Give her this. It's for the whole week. (*Thrusts some bills into* TERRY'S *hand.*)

TERRY. Linda, what's the matter! You're moving? Where?

LINDA. You bet I'm moving. Fast. And nobody'll *ever* know where. (LINDA *goes off* R.)

KEITH. What was that all about?

TERRY. What? . . . Oh, I don't know. She's a strange girl.

KEITH. Well, look, I've got to run. Gilman's waiting in the office for me. He's lining up a hell of a cast. And I'm going to meet Natalie Blake this evening. I'm having dinner with her and Gilman.

TERRY. Tonight! Keith, you're having dinner with father and me.

KEITH. Oh, for God's sake, Terry! I get a chance like this with a top manager, and a big star and you expect me to say, "I can't meet you tonight, I've got to have dinner with my girl and her father." That's what you want me to say, I suppose?

TERRY. No, no!

KEITH. I'll do the best I can. You know that. This whole thing is for you as much as for me. You know that, don't you?

TERRY. Yes.

KEITH. Well, then. Now, look, darling ——

(KAYE *comes in, and, seeing* TERRY, *halts in doorway. She is a figure of despair.*)

TERRY. Why, Kaye! What are you doing back?

KAYE. They let me out.

TERRY. Oh, Kaye!

KAYE. There was another girl rehearsing when I got there. I'm fired.

TERRY. But they can't do that! How long had you been rehearsing?

KAYE. They still could. This was the seventh day.

TERRY. Darling, don't let it upset you. It happens to all of us. (*A realization of her own recent disappointment comes over her.*) To me. It's part of this crazy business.

KAYE. Terry, I haven't a cent.

TERRY. Who cares! I've still got my radio job. We'll get along.

KAYE. (*Dully.*) Don't try to fool me. I know about the radio job. You've only got two more weeks. I can't take any more money from you. I owe you more than a hundred dollars.

TERRY. What of it! Now look. Come on. Have lunch with Dad and me. Come on down to my radio rehearsal.

KAYE. (*Starts for stairs.*) No, I couldn't, Terry, I just—couldn't. Don't you bother about me. I'm all right.

KEITH. It's tough.

TERRY. Oh, dear, I hate to leave you like this. Don't be low, darling.

KAYE. (*As she goes upstairs.*) I'm all right. Thanks, Terry. (*Exits.*)

TERRY. (*To KEITH.*) This meant everything to her.

KEITH. The season's just begun. She'll get something else. Now look, darling, you and your dad have a nice dinner some place and leave my ticket at the box-office and I'll be along just as soon as I can. Will you do that, Sweet?

TERRY. Yes.

KEITH. O. K.! That's my girl! You're the swellest kid that ever lived. (*He goes. Door slams.*)

(TERRY *stands for a moment, then moves* R. *to table. Looks upstairs, then at money in hand.* MATTIE *comes into room intent on tidying the ash trays, etc. She makes the rounds with an ash receptacle and dustcloth.*)

TERRY. Mattie, where's Mrs. Orcutt?

MATTIE. Back in her room.

(TERRY *goes in search of* MRS. ORCUTT. *Off up* L. MATTIE *hums a snatch of lively songs as she works about the room. A piercing scream of terror is heard from above stairs.* SUSAN *hurtles down*

61

*stairs, her face distorted with terror. Simultaneously,* TERRY
*rushes in.*)

TERRY. What is it! What is it!
SUSAN. Up in the hall. She drank something. She's ——
TERRY. No! No! (*Rushes upstairs followed by* MATTIE *as* MRS.
ORCUTT *and* FRANK *run on from up* L.)
MRS. ORCUTT. What's the matter? What happened? What happened?

. (SUSAN *motions upstairs and* MRS. ORCUTT *and* FRANK *run up.*)

TERRY. (*Upstairs.*) Kaye! Kaye! Can you
hear me?
MATTIE. (*Upstairs.*) Oh, Lord, look at her.
TERRY. Kaye, darling! Why did you do it!
MATTIE. Oh, look at her face.
TERRY. Here, let me hold her! Kaye!
MATTIE. Poor little lamb.                          (*Simultaneously*
MRS. OR. Oh, this is terrible!                     *in hushed tones.*)
FRANK. Want me to carry her in her room?
MATTIE. What'd she swallow? What was it?
FRANK. Here's the bottle. Don't say nothing
on it.
MRS. OR. I'll get a doctor.

(*During above dialogue* SUSAN *has dropped down slowly to piano,
where she sinks on bench sobbing.* MRS. ORCUTT *comes downstairs
quickly and goes to phone, dialing number, as she does so* TERRY
*comes down slowly.*)

TERRY. (*Coming into room.*) It's no use, she's ——
MRS. OR. (*Hangs up receiver.*) It'll be in all the papers. I never
should have let her stay here. I felt it from the start. There was
something about her. She was different from the rest of you.
TERRY. Don't say that! It might have been any one of us. She was
just a girl without a job like—it might have been any one of us.

### CURTAIN

# ACT II

SCENE 2: *The same. 7 o'clock in the evening, about two months later.*
*JUDITH'S hat and coat on piano at rise.*
*Again SAM is waiting for a tardy BOBBY. Obviously it has been a long wait and his patience is frayed. He peers upstairs, paces the room, crosses to piano and impatiently fingers a few notes of " Old Man River."*
*BOBBY floats downstairs, as Southern as ever.*

BOBBY. Hello, there, Honey Bun.
SAM. Hello, Sugar!
BOBBY. Ah didn't keep you waitin', did Ah?
SAM. No. No.
BOBBY. (*Fussing with his necktie.*) Just look at your tie! Ah declare, Ah don't see how Ah can keep on lovin' you, the way you get yourself up.
SAM. (*On their way out.*) Go on! Everybody knows you're crazy about me.
BOBBY. Ah sure enough am. Ah just can't sleep or eat.
SAM. Honest, Honey?
BOBBY. Mhm. . . . Where we going to have dinner?

(*They go, exit up R. TWO MARYS enter from dining room, crossing to stairs deep in an argument.*)

LITTLE M. Well, what do you want to do all evening? I'm sick of movies and you don't want to sit around *here*.
BIG M. I'll tell you what. Let's go and see Keith Burgess' play.
LITTLE M. Keith Burgess' play! We couldn't get into that. The paper says seats eight weeks in advance and fifty standees last night.

(*They start upstairs.*)

BIG M. Then two more won't matter. That's all we want to do—stand up.
LITTLE M. Yes, but I don't think we ought to ask.
BIG M. Good Lord, you don't want to *pay*, do you?
LITTLE M. Pay? For theatre? You must be out of your mind.

BIG M. Well, *some* people must pay.

(*Doorbell.* MATTIE *enters from dining room. Looks back.*)

MATTIE. Did you put a new 'lectric bulb up in Miss Kendall's room?
FRANK. (*Enters from dining room.*) I will.
MATTIE. Give Miss Terry that telephone message? From Mr. Kingsley.
FRANK. (*Entering.*) Land-sakes, I forgot.
MATTIE. Well, you better tell her—he's important. And you can close up the dining room—everybody's been in that's going to eat. (FRANK *closes dining room. At outer door.*) Well, I declare!

(*The reason for her exclamation becomes apparent as* KEITH *comes into the room. He is a figure of splendor in full evening regalia—white tie, top hat, white muffler, beautifully tailored top-coat.* MATTIE *goes toward stairs with her astonished gaze so fixed on this dazzling apparition as to make her ascent a somewhat stumbling one.* KEITH, *waiting, puts coat on* R. *bookcase, drops down* C., *takes out platinum-and-gold cigarette case, symbol of his seduction, taps a cigarette smartly, lights it.* JUDITH, *the last to finish her dinner, comes out of dining room eating a large banana. As* KEITH *bursts upon her vision she stops dead, and all progress with the banana is temporarily suspended.*)

KEITH. (*Removing his hat.*) Hello, Judith.

(JUDITH *advances slowly to him, grasps the hand that holds the hat, moves it up so that the hat is held at about shoulder height, backs up, lifts her skirts a little, and is about to kick when* KEITH, *outraged, breaks his position and walks away from her.*)

JUD. Well, if you don't want to play. (*Takes final bite of her banana.*)
KEITH. Pixie, eh?

(JUDITH *tosses banana skin on the floor between them, beckons him enticingly.*)

MATTIE. (*Descending stairs.*) Miss Terry'll be right down.

JUD. (*Shakes head dolefully as she picks up banana skin.*) You were more fun in the other costume.

KEITH. You'd better watch your figure, eating those bananas. Starches and show business don't go together.

JUD. (*Putting on coat which was on piano at rise.*) They do in my show. I got nothing to compete with but elephants.

KEITH. Are there idiots who really *go* to those childish things—pay money?

JUD. Say, you can't have *all* the idiots. You're doing pretty good; give us some of the overflow.

KEITH. I suppose you know we broke the house-record last week.

JUD. Oh, sure. I stayed up all Saturday night to get the returns.

KEITH. (*Under his breath.*) Wise-cracker.

(TERRY'S *voice is heard as she comes running downstairs.*)

TERRY. So-o-o sorry, Mr. Burgess! At the last minute I had a run in my stocking and I had to ——— (*She stops short down* C., *as she sees* KEITH'S *magnificent effect. She herself is wearing her every-day clothes.*)

JUD. (*Sensing trouble.*) Well, I'll—I'll leave you two young people together. (*She gives the effect of tiptoeing out of room, exits up* R.)

TERRY. (*Dazzled.*) Keith! (*She curtsies to the floor.*) Did you remember to bring the glass slipper?

KEITH. What's the idea, Terry? I told you on the phone we were dressing.

TERRY. I thought you were joking. You said, "We'll dress, of couse," and I said, "Of course!" But I didn't dream you were serious.

KEITH. We're going to an opening night! And our seats are third row center!

TERRY. Downstairs?

KEITH. Down ——— Where do you think?

TERRY. Darling, we've been to openings before, and we always sat in the gallery.

KEITH. Gallery! We're through with the gallery! I've got a table at Twenty One for dinner, and after the theatre we're invited to a party at Gilman's pent-house. You can't go like that!

TERRY. (*As she starts for stairs.*) Give me just ten minutes—I'll go up and change. (*She suddenly recollects—stops.*) Oh, **dear!**

KEITH. What's the matter?

TERRY. I loaned my evening dress to Susan.

KEITH. Oh, for God's —— (*Turns away in disgust.*)

TERRY. (*Starts again.*) It's all right. I'll borrow Judy's pink ——
(*Stops.*) Oh, no! Olga's wearing it.

KEITH. (*Crossing* L.) This is the damnedest dump I was ever in!
Sordid kind of life! Wearing each other's clothes! I suppose you
use each other's toothbrushes, too!

TERRY. (*Quietly.*) Would you rather I didn't go, Keith?

KEITH. I didn't say that I ——

TERRY. (*Still quietly.*) Yes—but would you rather?

KEITH. Now you're playing it for tragedy. What's the matter with
you, anyhow!

TERRY. (*Drops down* C.) There's nothing the matter with me,
Keith. I just can't see us as third-row first-nighters. We always
went to see the *play*, Keith. That whole crowd—it makes the
audience more important than the show.

KEITH. Listen, I don't like those people any better than you do.
They don't mean anything to *me*.

TERRY. Then why do you bother with them?

KEITH. They can't *hurt* me. I watch them as you'd watch a hill of
ants. Insects, that's what they are.

TERRY. Keith, listen, you wrote your last play about people you
understood and liked. You lived with them, and you knew them,
and they gave you something. You'll starve to death in third row
center.

KEITH. I'm going back to them. I'm no fool. They're keeping my
room for me just as it was.

TERRY. Keeping it? How do you mean?

KEITH. Oh, I don't want to talk about it now. Come on, let's get
out of here.

TERRY. But I've got to know. Do you mean you've moved without
even telling me?

KEITH. (*Decides to face the music, crosses to couch* R.) Well, I
was going to break it to you later. I knew you'd jump on me. But
as long as you've gone this far—I'm going to Hollywood.

TERRY. Hollywood!

KEITH. Yes, to write for pictures.

TERRY. No, no, Keith!

KEITH. Now don't start all over again! If you don't watch yourself
you'll turn into one of those nagging —— (*He stops as* KENDALL
*comes downstairs.*)

66

*(She is dressed for the street. Throws a glance into the room, in passing, and notices* KEITH'S *unusual attire.)*

KEN. *(Impressed, very friendly.)* Hel-lo!

KEITH. *(With no cordiality.)* H'are you?

KEN. *(Senses she has walked into a hornets' nest.)* Good-bye. *(Beats a hasty retreat via front door up* R.)

KEITH. Let's get out of here.

TERRY. Keith, you can't go to Hollywood! I won't let you! You said you'd never go no matter how broke you were, and now that your play's a big hit you're going. Why? Why?

KEITH. Well, they didn't want me *before* it was a hit.

TERRY. Keith, listen ——

KEITH. I know what you're going to say. All that junk about its shriveling up my soul. Listen! I'm going to use Hollywood. It's not going to use me. I'm going to stay one year at two thousand a week. That's one hundred thousand dollars. I'll write their garbage in the daytime, but at night I'll write my own plays.

TERRY. But *will* you? That's what I'm afraid of. *Will* you?

KEITH. You bet I will! And in between I'll keep fit with sunshine, and swimming, and tennis, and ——

TERRY. Little ermine jackets, up to here.

KEITH. Huh?

TERRY. It doesn't matter.

KEITH. Believe me, they'll never catch me at their Trocaderos or their Brown Derbies.

TERRY. *(Quietly.)* When are you going, Keith?

KEITH. I don't know. Next week.

TERRY. Well—good-bye.

KEITH. What!

TERRY. Good-bye, Keith, and good luck. It's been swell. *(She turns, runs swiftly upstairs.)*

*(*KEITH *goes to foot of stairs and calls.)*

KEITH. Terry! What's the —— Terry! . . . Terry! Terry!

*(Only silence from above. He claps his hat on his head, and goes. Door slams loudly after him. Immediately on the slam of the door* BERNICE *tiptoes downstairs with a catlike swiftness and soundlessness. Obviously she has been eavesdropping. A quick comprehen-*

*sive look around the room, then she scurries to window, peers out guardedly, so as not to be seen from the street. Turns back from window just as the* TWO MARYS *make swift silent descents. The three at once plunge into an elaborate pantomimic routine revealing their knowledge of the scene which has just taken place between* TERRY *and* KEITH, *and their unbounded interests in its consequences.*)

BIG M. (*Whispered.*) Is he gone?

BERN. Yes. How's Terry?

LITTLE M. She's in her room.

BERN. Do you think she can hear us?

BIG M. She might.

LITTLE M. Wasn't it terrible?

BERN. I thought I'd die.

LITTLE M. Poor Terry.

BIG M. I never did like him.

BERN. Me neither.            (*Whispering.*)

LITTLE M. We'd better go back up or she'll be suspicious.

(*They start upstairs.*)

BIG M. Yes, be very quiet.

BERN. Shall we ask her if we can do anything?

BIG M. No.

(*Doorbell rings, they vanish upstairs.* FRANK *appears, getting into his housecoat and casting a resentful glance back at the unseen* MATTIE. *As door is opened the voice of* KINGSLEY *is heard:* " *Does Miss Terry Randall happen to be in?* " FRANK: " *Yessuh, I think so. Will you come right in?* " FRANK *comes into sight.* " *What's the name, suh?* ")

KINGSLEY. Mr. Kingsley.

FRANK. Oh, yeh. You the gentleman telephoned. I clean forgot to tell Miss Terry.

KINGS. Well, as long as she's here . . .

FRANK. Yessuh. (*Pulls himself together and goes upstairs.* KINGSLEY *comes into the room. He stands a moment, then takes out cigarette case and lights cigarette.* FRANK *comes down again.*) I told her you was here.

KINGS. Oh, thank you.

68

FRANK. And I told her about the phone call, too. (FRANK *goes about his business as* TERRY *comes downstairs.*)

TERRY. (*To him* C., *shakes hands.*) Why, Mr. Kingsley, how dramatic! You're just in the nick of time.

KINGS. I'm glad of that. What's happened?

TERRY. (*Starts* R. *to couch.*) Oh—sort of an emotional crisis. I dashed upstairs to have a good cry, buried my head in the pillow just the way you're supposed to, and guess what?

KINGS. What?

TERRY. The tears wouldn't come. In fact, I felt sort of relieved and light, as though I'd just got over a fever.

KINGS. How disappointing. Like not being able to sneeze.

TERRY. Perhaps I'll be able to manage it later. Tonight.

KINGS. If a shoulder would be of any—help?

TERRY. No, thanks. I'm afraid I have to work this out alone. . . . (*Sits on couch.*) Do take your coat off.

KINGS. (*Takes off coat, drops it in armchair* L.) Thanks. This is rather a strange hour for me to drop in. I did telephone ——

TERRY. Oh, Frank doesn't believe in phone messages.

KINGS. (*Crossing to couch.*) They do in Hollywood. They just called me up. Can you take a plane for California tomorrow?

TERRY. Me! (*He murmurs an assent.*) What for?

KINGS. They didn't say what the part was—sort of character-comedy, I believe. Of course they put the picture in production first and then started looking for a cast—the Alice-in-Wonderland method. At any rate, they want a new face in this particular part; they ran off all the screen tests they had on file, and finally came to that one of yours. So there you are. And—oh, yes—they want to know in twenty minutes. Of course it's only four-thirty on the Coast.

TERRY. You're joking.

KINGS. No, all important things are decided in twenty minutes out there. The more trivial ones take years. Shall I phone them you'll be there?

TERRY. Why—I don't know.

KINGS. You don't mean to say you're hesitating!

TERRY. But it's so fantastic! How can I ——?

KINGS. (*Sitting next to* TERRY.) Dear child, do you mind if I tell you something ? (TERRY *looks up at him.*) I've been watching you for several seasons. You've been in the theatre for two—three— what is it?

TERRY. Three.

KINGS. Three years. You've appeared in, perhaps, half a dozen plays. I wouldn't call any of them exactly hits—would you? (TERRY *merely shakes her head.*) And one or two of them closed before the week was over.

TERRY. You've been doing a lot of detective work.

KINGS. No, I didn't need to. I know all about you.

TERRY. You do! That's a little frightening.

KINGS. It's part of my business—watching the good ones. And you are good. You've got fire and variety and a magnetic quality that's felt the minute you walk on a stage.

TERRY. (*As he hesitates.*) Oh, don't stop!

KINGS. But off stage you're nothing at all. (TERRY *wishes she had left well enough alone.*) When you walk into an office the average manager doesn't see anything there. You might be the little girl who's come to deliver the costumes. They wouldn't see that spark. If Elizabeth Bergner walked in on them unknown—or Helen Hayes—what would they see! Little anæmic wisps that look as if they could do with a sandwich and a glass of milk. But put them on a stage, and it's as if you had lighted a thousand incandescent bulbs behind their eyes. That's talent—that's acting—that's you!

TERRY. Now I—*am* going to cry.

KINGS. But what if they don't see what's hidden in you? Suppose they never see it. You might go tramping around for twenty years, and never get your chance. That's the stage.

TERRY. Twenty years!

KINGS. (*Rises, pulls* TERRY *up.*) But let's say you go to Hollywood. They'll know what to do with you out there. Light you so as to fill those hollows, only take your—(*He is turning her head this way and that to get the best angle.*) right profile. That's the good one. Shade the nose a trifle. (*Opens her mouth and peers in as though she were a race horse.*) Perhaps a celluloid cap over those two teeth. Yes, they'd make you very pretty. (TERRY *steals a quick look in mirror. Her morale is somewhat shaken.*) Then you play in this picture. Fifty million people see you. Fan mail. Next time you get a better part. No tramping up and down Broadway, no worries about money. A seven-year contract, your salary every week whether you work or not. And if you make a really big hit, like Jean, they'll tear up your contract and give you a better one.

TERRY. (*A sudden idea.*) Wouldn't they let me do just one or two pictures, instead of this seven-year thing?

KINGS. I'm afraid not. If you make a big hit they don't want another studio to reap the benefit. That's not unreasonable, is it?

TERRY. (*As she crosses* L.) No, I suppose not. Oh, dear! Everything you say is absolutely sound and true, but you see, Mr. Kingsley, the trouble with me is—I'm stagestruck. The theatre beats me and starves me and forsakes me, but I love it. I suppose that's the kind of girl I am—you know—rather live in a garret with her true love than dwell in a palace with old Money-bags.

KINGS. (*Moving in* C.) But it looks as though your true love had kicked you out of the garret.

TERRY. Oh, dear, if there was just somebody. Mr. Kingsley, won't *you* help me? Won't you tell me what to do?

KINGS. Me?

TERRY. Please!

KINGS. But I work for the picture company.

TERRY. But if you didn't?

KINGS. (*Quietly*.) I'd think you ought to tell them to go to hell.

TERRY. What!

KINGS. (*Indignantly*.) Go out there and let them do all those things to you! (*Again he has a finger under her chin, raising her head as he scans her face*.) That lovely little face! And for what? So that a few years from now they can throw you out on the ash-heap! The theatre may be slow and heart-breaking, but if you build solidly you've got something at the end of seven years, and seventeen years, and twenty-seven! Look at Katharine Cornell, and Lynn Fontanne and Alfred Lunt. They tramped Broadway in their day. They've worked like horses, and trouped the country, and stuck to it. And now they've got something that nothing in the world can take away from them. And what's John Barrymore got? A yacht!

TERRY. You're wonderful!

KINGS. Are you going to Hollywood?

TERRY. No!

KINGS. Will you go to dinner?

TERRY. YES!

KINGS. That's really all I came to ask you.

TERRY. Just a minute, I'll get my hat. (*Runs for stairs as curtain falls*.)

## CURTAIN

# ACT III

SCENE 1: *Same. A Sunday morning. The following October.*

*The girls are scattered about room in various informal attitudes and various stages of attire. Pajamas, lounging robes, hair-nets, cold cream, wave-combs. Four or five Sunday papers, opened and distributed among the girls, are in drifts everywhere, girls are lying on the floor reading bits of this and that, lounging in chairs, coffee cups, bits of toast, a banana or an orange show that Sunday morning breakfast is a late and movable feast.*

KENDALL *is in riding clothes and bound for a day in the country. All the girls are present except* TERRY.

*During the year two new girls have joined the club, and now are sprawled at ease with the others.*

OLGA, *at piano, is obliging with the latest popular tune.* MADELEINE *rather absent-mindedly sings a fragment of the song, leaving a word half-finished as her attention is momentarily held by something she is reading. A foot is waggled in time to the music.* PAT, *sprawled full-length on top of grand piano, is giving a rather brilliant performance of dancing with her legs in the air.*

LITTLE MARY, *on hands and knees, is making a tour of the recumbent figures in search of a certain theatrical news item. In one hand she holds a half-eaten banana.*

LITTLE M. (*Crawling from* C. *to* D. L.) Where's the list of next week's openings? (*She finds that* BIG MARY, *lying on floor* L., *has the page she wants. She settles down to read over her shoulder.*)

BOBBY. (*Sitting on arch bookcase* L.) Anybody got a roll they don't want?

TONY GILLETTE. (*One of the new girls, sitting on* R. *end of couch.*) Here!

BOBBY. Toss!

(*The muffin is hurled through the air.*)

MAD. (*Lying full-length stage* R. C. *Turning a page of rotogravure section.*) Autumn Millinery Modes. Oh, look at the hats they're going to wear!

(OLGA *stops playing.*)

SUSAN. (*From behind* L. *end of couch.*) Let me see. (*Traverses the distance to* MADELEINE *by two neat revolutions of her entire body, and brings up just behind the outspread papers. Reads:*) Paris says " Hats will be worn off the head this winter."

PAT. (*On piano. Suspended in mid-air as her attention is caught by this remark.*) Where?

SUSAN. That's what it says. " Hats'll be worn off the head this winter."

BERN. (*At the desk* R.) Where're they going to put 'em?

LITTLE M. (OLGA *starts playing* Für Elise. *Busy with the American.*) Did you know that in Ancient Egypt five thousand years ago the women used to dye their hair just like we do?

JUD. (*Seated in armchair* L. *Furious.*) Who's we?

BIG M. (*To* LITTLE MARY, *who is reading over her shoulder.*) Take that banana out of my face, will you!

(SUSAN *crawls over to* ELLEN, *lying* R. *of* JUDITH.)

ELLEN FENWICK. (*The other new girl. Perusing the department store ads.*) " Two-piece Schiaparelli suits—$5.98. You cannot tell the model from the copy."

JUD. The hell you can't.

SUSAN. (*Emerging from newspaper.*) Oh, they're postponing that " Lord Byron " play because they can't find a leading man.

LITTLE M. What are they looking for?

SUSAN. He's got to be young and handsome.

ELLEN. There are no handsome men on the stage any more.

JUD. There's a shortage off stage, too.

PAT. Looks don't count any more. It's good old sex appeal.

(OLGA *stops playing.*)

KEN. Would you rather go out with a handsome man without sex appeal, or a homely man *with* it?

BERN. I'd rather go out with the handsome one.

73

JUD. Sure, and stay *in* with the other one.

ANN. (*Who has been seated over* R. *rises as* JUDITH'S *sally is greeted with a general laugh.*) I think you girls are simply disgusting!! Men, men, men! It's degrading just to listen to you. (*As she moves up to* L. *of desk.*)

JUD. *Isn't* it, though?

BIG M. Say, Terry! . . . Where's Terry?

JUD. She's still asleep. It's the only chance she gets—Sundays.

BIG M. I see that old beau of hers is coming back.

(OLGA *starts Chopin's C Sharp Minor Waltz.*)

TONY. Who's that?

BIG M. Keith Burgess. He used to hang around here all the time.

TONY. Really? What's he like?

JUD. He's one of those fellows started out on a soapbox and ended up in a swimming pool.

LITTLE M. Terry was crazy about him, all right.

BIG M. Yeah.

PAT. And if you ask me, I think she still is.

LITTLE M. Really! What makes you think so?

PAT. Somebody just mentioned his name the other day and you ought to've seen her face!

JUD. She's forgotten he ever lived—that Left-Wing Romeo.

KEN. Well, I should think she might, with David Kingsley in the offing. Now, I call *him* attractive!

PAT. Oh, Kingsley isn't her type. Anyway, he's just interested in her career.

KEN. If it's just her career they eat an awful lot of dinners together.

LITTLE M. If it's art he's got on his mind why doesn't he get her a job? Not much of a career standing behind a sales-counter.

BOBBY. Yes, Ah think it's perfectly awful the way Terry has to get up at half-past seven every morning. That miserable job of hers.

MAD. It's no worse than what I've got ahead of me.

SUSAN. Well, anyway, you'll be acting.

MAD. (*Rising, crossing to chair* R.) Acting! A Number Three Company of "A Horse on You," playing up and down the West Coast. God! I came to New York to get away from Seattle, and they keep shipping me back there. (*Sits* R.)

BOBBY. You'll be earning some money! Look at Sam and me! We

·an't make enough to get married. Ah declare Ah'm so bored with
livin' in sin.

(OLGA *stops playing.*)

ANN. Well, really!
LITTLE M. Oh, shut up!
JUD. Speaking of Seattle, Miss Vauclain, would you be good
enough to take that load of lumber off my neck! After all, you
put it there.
MAD. It isn't my fault if he fell for you.
PAT. Oh, is Lumber in town again?
JUD. No; but I've had a warning. (*Drawing letter from her pa-
jama pocket.*)
ANN. (*Impatiently, rising.* OLGA *starts Debussy's First Arabesque.*)
Oh, I'm not going to waste my whole Sunday! What time is Jean
coming?
MAD. Stick around. What have you got to lose?
ANN. My time's just as valuable as Jean's is.
MAD. Sure. You're in big demand. Sit down.
ANN. Well, if Jean wants to see me I'm upstairs. (OLGA *stops play-
ing.*) This conversation isn't very uplifting. (ANN *goes upstairs.*)
OLGA. She should be teaching school, that girl. (*Starts playing
Beethoven Sonata in D Minor.*)
TONY. Is Jean Maitland as pretty off the screen as she is on? I've
never seen her.
ELLEN. Neither have I.
KEN. She's much better looking off. They've made her up like all
the rest of them on the screen.

(OLGA *stops playing.*)

OLGA. I hope she will soon be here. I must be at the Winter Garden
at one o'clock.
LITTLE M. On Sunday!
OLGA. (*Bitterly.*) On Sunday. (*Goes into a few bars of the newest
Winter Garden melody. Something very corny.*)
LITTLE M. Yeah, we know. Kolijinsky.

(*A voice which we later find is that of* LOUISE MITCHELL HENDER-
SHOT *calls out from dining room.*)

75

LOUISE. Olga!

OLGA. What is it?

LOUISE. What's that you're playing?

OLGA. (*Not very clearly heard above the music.*) "Hill-billy Sam."

LOUISE. (*Off.*) What?

OLGA. Ah! Come in here if you want to talk.

PAT. Yes, stop stuffing yourself and come in here . . . Heh, Louise!

LOUISE. (*As she comes out of dining room.*) I was having some pancakes. (*Crossing to* C.)

PAT. Listen, you've got to cut out those farmhand breakfasts. now that you're back in New York.

LOUISE. (*Settles herself in the group* C.) Imagine getting the *Times* the day it's printed instead of three days later!

JUD. You mean you're not lonesome for good old Appleton?

LOUISE. I haven't been so happy in years. (*She turns her attention to the paper.*)

JUD. Everything pink, eh?

BIG M. (OLGA *plays E Major Brahms Waltz.*) Oh, say, Irene Fitzroy has been engaged for the society girl part in " River House."

(*A series of highly interested responses to this.*)

SUSAN. No! . . . Really! . . .

KEN. That's wonderful!

LITTLE M. She'll be good in it! . . .

LOUISE. Isn't it exciting!

BERN. (*As she rises from desk.*) I could have played that Fitzroy part. I don't know why I couldn't be a society girl. (*Assumes a supercilious expression to prove her fitness for the part. A chorus of:*)

PAT. Sure! . . . We know . . .

LITTLE M. You're always the type.

BERN. A real actress can play anything. I may play the French adventuress in " Love and War."

(OLGA *stops playing. A little chorus of astonishment:* ALL *turn to her.*)

LITTLE M. Really!

BIG M. No kidding!

KEN. Do you mean they offered it to you?

BERN. Well, not exactly, but I'm writing 'em a letter. (*Back to desk, sits.*)

(*Another chorus:*)

PAT. Oh, we see . . .

(OLGA *starts E Flat Major Nocturne of Chopin.*)

KEN. Letters! . . .

MAD. You and your letters!

(MATTIE *comes out of dining room with large tray. She is intent on gathering up coffee cups.*)

MATTIE. You-all knows Mrs. Orcutt don't allow you girls to go laying around downstairs in your pajamas.

(LOUISE *rises, gives* MATTIE *two cups, then goes up to* L. *arch.*)

JUD. (*Dreamily, as she reads.*) Don't give it another thought, Mattie. We'll take 'em right off.

(MADELEINE *rises and up to* L. *of desk.*)

MATTIE. Besides, look-it this here room! Banana skins and newspapers and toast! I should think with Miss Jean coming you'd be getting all slicked up. Big moving picture star. (*Takes a grapefruit off a small piece of statuary, where it has been draped as a hat. She goes back to dining room with her laden tray.*)

(*For a second there is a lull as the* GIRLS *are absorbed in their papers.*)

MAD. (*To* BERNICE.) Are you still writing that letter about yourself?

BERN. (*Rises and down a bit.*) Look. How many X's are there in sexy?

MAD. Why don't you give up, anyhow?

BIG M. Yeh, why don't you take up ballet-dancing, or something?

BERN. (*Springs suddenly to her feet, her hands clutching back of chair behind her.* OLGA *stops playing.*) Don't you say that to me. I'm never going to give up. Why, I'm as good as —— (*She realizes she is making a spectacle of herself.*) Leave me alone. (*Back to desk, sits.*)

KEN. (SUSAN *rises and sits* R. *end of table.*) Ah, they were just kidding. Can't you take a joke?

(OLGA *starts* A Flat Major Brahms Waltz. TERRY *runs down stairs, stopping halfway to toss a word of greeting to the girls below.*)

TERRY. (*A gesture that embraces them all.*) Ah! My public!

LOUISE. Hello.

BOBBY. H'ya!

JUD. Well, Terry, the Beautiful Shop-Girl.

PAT. Thought you were never going to get up.

TERRY. I wouldn't, if it weren't for Jean's coming. . . . Heh, Mattie! (*A "Yes'm," from* MATTIE *in dining room.*) Draw one in the dark! . . . Oh, isn't Sunday heavenly! (*Stretches luxuriantly.*) I woke up at half-past seven; said, "Nope, I don't have to," and went right back to sleep. Not all day long do I have to say, "This blouse is a copy of a little import that we are selling for $3.95. I am sure you would look simply terrible in it." (*Sits* L. *arm of couch.*)

JUD. I'm going to come down there some day and have you wait on me.

TERRY. If you do I'll have you pinched for shoplifting.

BOBBY. (*Getting off bookcase, drops down* C.) Honest, Terry, Ah don't see how you tolerate that job of yours. Moochin' down there nine o'clock in the mawnin'. Slaving till six, and after.

TERRY. Oh, it isn't so terrible if you keep thinking that next week that part will turn up. I keep on making the rounds.

ELLEN. But when do you have time for it?

TERRY. Lunch hour.

SUSAN. Then when do you eat lunch?

TERRY. Sundays.

(BOBBY *exits in dining room.*)

PAT. (*Getting off piano, starts for stairs.*) Just goes to show how cuckoo the stage is. You can act rings around all of us. Well—

(*Stretching a bit as she makes for stairs.*) I guess I'll go up and put the face together. I look like an old popover. (*Going up.*)

SUSAN. Me, too. Don't say anything good while we're gone. (*As she goes upstairs with* PAT.)

JUD. What are you going to do today, Terry, after Jean goes?

(BOBBY *comes on and goes to piano* L.)

TERRY. I don't know. Who's doing what? Kendall, you're going social for the day, h'm?

KEN. Yes, I'm going out to Piping Rock.

TERRY. Piping Rock—isn't that where your ancestors landed?

KEN. Thereabouts.

JUD. Mine landed in Little Rock.

BIG M. Oh, say, Terry! The paper says Keith Burgess gets back from the Coast today. Did you know that?

(*A little hush. The eyes of the girls are turned toward* TERRY.)

TERRY. Yes, I know. Why do they call California the Coast instead of New York?

LITTLE M. I wonder if that sunshine has mellowed him up any.

BOBBY. (*Holding up paper.*) Girls, here's Jean stepping out of an airplane!

(OLGA *stops playing.*)

BERN. (*Jumping up.*) Oh, let's see it. (*To* BOBBY *at piano.*)

BOBBY. (*As three or four girls cluster around her including* TERRY. *Reads:*) "Blond Hollywood Screen Star Alights at Newark Airport."

LITTLE M. That's a darling costume!

BIG M. I don't like her hat.

BERN. (*Takes paper, crosses* R. *to window. Reading.*) "Lovely Jean Maitland, Popular Screen Actress, Arrives for Rehearsals of Broadway Stage Play."

JUD. That belle certainly is shot with luck.

BOBBY. That's what she is! (*As she crosses* R. *to table.*)

JUD. First she goes out and knocks 'em cold in pictures, and now she gets starred on Broadway.

BIG M. And she isn't even a good actress.

(MATTIE *brings* TERRY'S *coffee from dining room.*)

MATTIE. (*In dining room door.*) Here's your coffee, Miss Terry.
TERRY. Thanks, Mattie.
ELLEN. What's she going to do? Quit pictures and stay on the stage?
BIG M. No, no. The picture company puts on the play. It's like a personal appearance.
BERN. (*Who has drifted over to window.*) Girls! She's here!
BIG M. (*Darting to window.*) Let's see!

(*A wild scramble to tidy the room. Newspapers, cigarette butts, etc.*)

BOBBY. Look at that car, would you!
LOUISE. Isn't it gorgeous!
LITTLE M. There she is! She's getting out!
BERN. Oohoo! (*Raps on window.*) Jean!

(*With a concerted rush they make for front door.*)

(*NOTE: Lines A to B are read simultaneously as girls rush out in hall to meet* JEAN *and as those remaining in room tidy it up.*)

(A) BOBBY. She looks marvelous, doesn't she!
BIG M. I wonder if she's changed!
BERN. Isn't it exciting!
TONY. Don't forget to introduce me!
ELLEN. Yes. Me, too!
LOUISE. (*Calling upstairs.*) Girls! Yoohoo! She's here!

(*Meanwhile, on the part of the remaining girls, there is a wild scramble to tidy up room.*)

LITTLE M. She's got on Red Foxes. (*Cue for* TERRY *to speak.*)
TERRY. Here—pick up the papers! Give them to me! (*With a great bundle of newspapers she dashes into dining room and out again.*)
MAD. We should have got all dressed up.
JUD. Not me. She's seen me worse than this.

OLGA. She will be dressed up enough.
KEN. We're acting like a lot of school girls. We'll be asking for her autograph next.

(*The squealing in hallway now mounts to a burst of ecstatic greeting.*)

LITTLE M. Jean! Jean!
BERN. DAR-ling!
LOUISE. WON-derful!
BIG M. Look grand!
BOBBY. Jean! Welcome home!
JEAN. (*Still in hallway.*) Oh, I'm so excited! How darling of you all to be here!

(SUSAN *and* PAT *run downstairs. From among the group:*)

LOUISE. Are you glad to be back?
(B) LITTLE M. You haven't changed a bit.

(JEAN *comes into view. Her costume is simple and horribly expensive. Her fox furs are fabulous, her orchids are pure white.*)

JEAN. (*Embracing girls.*) Hello, girls! Madeleine! Olga, how's the music? Kendall!! Hello, Judy. This is worth the whole trip ——

(TERRY *comes from dining room.*)

TERRY. Jean, darling!
JEAN. Terry!

(*They embrace.*)

MRS. OR. (*Looming up in the dining room doorway,* FRANK *and* MATTIE *just behind her.*) Well, well! My little Jean!
JEAN. Hello, Mrs. Orcutt! Mattie! Frank! (*In turn she throws her arms around all three of them. As she embraces* FRANK *a laugh goes up from the group.*) Well, let me get my breath and have a look at all of you.
BERN. It's the same old bunch. (*Grabs* JEAN'S *furs, runs to mirror down* R.)

TERRY. No, there are two new ones. Ellen Fenwick and Tony Gillette. Miss Jean Maitland.

TONY. Hello.

PAT. (*The trumpet sound.*) Ta-da-a-ah!

JEAN. Hello, girls. I hope you don't think I'm crazy—all excited like this.

ELLEN. Oh, no!

TONY. We think you're darling.

(BERNICE, *before mirror, is having a private try-on of* JEAN'S *fox and orchids. Enchanting effect.*)

ANN. Hello, Jean!

JEAN. (*In greeting to* ANN, *who has come rather sedately downstairs.*) Ann! I was just going to ask for you.

ANN. My, you look Hollywood!

BERN. Do you think it goes with my coloring?

BIG M. Let me try it.

JEAN. (*Recalls two men who have accompanied her, and who are standing in hallway. One has a huge camera and tripod.*) Oh, boys, I'm so sorry. Girls, this is Mr. Larry Westcott, our New York publicity man—and a wonder. And this is Billy—uh—I'm afraid I never heard your last name.

BILLY. Just Billy.

LARRY. Just want to snap a few pictures. Do you mind?

MRS. OR. (*A hand straightening her coiffure.*) Not at all.

LARRY. Human interest stuff.

BERN. You mean with us!

JEAN. Of course!

BOBBY. Oh, I've got to go and fix up.

(*A chorus of:*)

LOUISE. So do I!

LITTLE M. I look a fright.

BERN. Me, too!

BIG M. We won't be a minute.

(*Up the stairs go* BERNICE, BIG *and* LITTLE MARY, BOBBY *and* LOUISE. MATTIE *is doing a little sprucing up, preparatory to being photographed, and* FRANK *buttons his housecoat.*)

JEAN. Well, Terry!

TERRY. Jean, darling, aren't you thrilled at doing a play? When do your rehearsals start?

JEAN. (*Abstracted.*) On Wednesday.

BILLY. (*Speaking to* MRS. ORCUTT *and the two servants. He has his electric apparatus in his hand.*) I've got a pretty strong light here. All right if I plug in?

FRANK. Yes, sah. I'll show you.

(BILLY *and* FRANK *disappear into hallway toward rear of house.*)

LARRY. Pardon me, Miss Maitland. You were going to ask about our taking some shots upstairs. (*Glancing from* JEAN *to* MRS. ORCUTT.)

JEAN. Oh, yes. Do you mind, Mrs. Orcutt? They want to take some stills of me up in my old room.

MRS. OR. Of course not.

LARRY. You know—Humble Beginnings in The Footlights Club. They love it.

MRS. OR. Why, yes, I'd be delighted.

TERRY. Wait a minute! I've got my Sunday wash hanging up there. You can't photograph that!

LARRY. Great! Just what we want!

TERRY. All right. But I never thought my underwear would make Screenland.

OLGA. So you are a big actress now, eh, Jean? You are going to be starred in a play.

JEAN. Isn't it silly! I didn't really want them to star me in it. I'm scared stiff.

LARRY. She'll be great. Look, Miss Maitland, we haven't got a lot of time. Mr. Kingsley is picking you up here at twelve forty-five and then you're meeting Mr. Gretzl.

TERRY. Who?

JEAN. Mr. Gretzl.

JUD. What's a Gretzl?

JEAN. He's the Big Boss—Adolph Gretzl.

LARRY. President of the Company.

MRS. OR. Of course! Adolph Gretzl.

OLGA. (*Dashing to piano. Improvises and sings.*)
Of course Adolph Gretzl,
He looks like a pretzl ——

83

JUD. (*Picking it up.*)
                    So why should we fretzl ——
PAT. And fume. Boom-boom. (*She times last with a couple of bumps.*)

(*The* TWO MARYS *come dashing downstairs.*)

LITTLE M. We're ready!
LARRY. Okay! Everybody here now?
BIG M. Oh, no. There's more yet. Girls! Hurry!

(LOUISE'S *voice from upstairs:* " Coming!")

JEAN. Terry, darling, when am I going to see you? I've got loads to tell you and I want to hear all about you. Let's see—rehearsals start Wednesday. How about lunch tomorrow?
LARRY. Oh, not tomorrow, Miss Maitland. You're lunching with the Press.
JEAN. Oh, dear. Let's see—I'm going to that opening tomorrow night with David Kingsley. . . . How about tea?
LARRY. Not tea! You've got the magazine people. And you've got photographs all day Tuesday.
JEAN. (*Turns to* TERRY.) But I want to see her. How about Wednesday? I'll get away from rehearsal and we'll have lunch. One o'clock?
TERRY. You won't believe it, but my lunch hour's eleven-thirty to twelve-thirty.
JEAN. Eleven-thirty! What do you mean?

(*Down come* BOBBY *and* LOUISE *refurbished.*)

LOUISE. Are we late?
BOBBY. Ah hope we didn't keep you waitin'.
LARRY. (*Impatiently glancing at his watch.*) All right, Miss Maitland.
JEAN. Oh, fine. Now before we start, everybody, I've got a tweentsy-weentsy surprise for you.
BIG M. Surprise?
JEAN. Billy, will you bring it in?

(BILLY *goes into hall.*)

BOBBY. Bring what in?

LOUISE. What?

JEAN. It's for all of you, dear Mrs. Orcutt and the whole dear Footlights Club.

(BILLY *enters from hallway carrying what is evidently a large picture, framed and covered with a rich red drapery which conceals the subject.*)

BOBBY. Oh, look!

KEN. Oh, how exciting!

PAT. What is it?

TONY. Looks like a picture.

LITTLE M. What of, I wonder?

JUD. Papa Gretzl.

JEAN. All right, girls?

BOBBY. We're ready!

(LARRY *has placed picture on a chair, upright.* JEAN *steps forward, and with a sweeping gesture throws aside velvet drape. It is a portrait of* JEAN. *All eyelashes, golden hair and scarlet lips. A series of delighted and semi-delighted exclamations:*)

PAT. It's Jean!

ELLEN. Lovely!

TONY. How beautiful!

BOBBY. Darling.

(JUDITH: *a snap of the fingers.*)

MRS. OR. (*Her dismayed glance sweeping the walls.*) It's lovely, Jean, lovely! Now, if we can only find a fitting place to hang it.

LARRY. Well, let's see. (*With a look that alights on the Bernhardt portrait and rests there.*)

JUD. So long, Sarah! (JUDITH *makes a gallant gesture of Hail and Farewell toward the portrait of the Divine Sarah.*)

LARRY. Now, if you'll all just gather around the picture. . . . Okay, Billy!

BILLY. (*Who has been glimpsed now and then busy with his apparatus.*) Okay! Ready in a second.

85

LARRY. Now then, Miss Maitland. You right there behind the portrait and you, Mrs.—er —— (*Snaps finger at* MRS. ORCUTT.) Yes, right here beside Miss Maitland. Now you girls fill in here, making a little circle.

BIG M. Sure.

LARRY. And look toward Miss Maitland. That's right—all of you right in here. You, too, girls. That's right, you, too, girlie. We want a nice little informal group. No, you'll all have to crouch down. Everybody down. You, too, sister. (*This to* MRS. ORCUTT, *who gets down painfully.*) That's fine. And all looking at Miss Maitland.

JEAN. (*Very sweet.*) Frank and Mattie have to be in it. Come on, Frank and Mattie!

(*They have been looking a little crestfallen and now take their places at extreme edge, much elated.*)

LARRY. Sure, sure! It wouldn't be a picture without 'em. We want the whole Twilight Club. Now then, have we got everybody? (*Looks over his shoulder just as* BILLY *turns on his special light.*)

LITTLE M. No, no, where's Bernice?

BIG M. Bernice isn't here!

BERN. (*Her voice from top of stairs.*) I'm ready! Here I am! (BERNICE *has seized this opportunity to register as undiscovered Hollywood star material. She has made herself up to look like a rather smudged copy of Joan Crawford. Her entrance is undulating and regal.*)

PAT. Heh! That's my new dress!

BERN. Well, I had to be right, didn't I?

LARRY. Come on, girlie. Right here. (*Pushes her to her knees. Immediately* BERNICE *stares out toward camera.*) No, no! Look at Miss Maitland. Everybody look at Miss Maitland. And remember this will all be in the papers tomorrow.—Ready, Billy?

BILLY. Okay.

LARRY. Hold still now. And everybody look at Miss Maitland! Right! (*Just as* BILLY *squeezes bulb* BERNICE *makes a lightning full-face turn toward camera, all smiles, and back again before they can fairly accuse her of it.*) Now then for the pictures upstairs. . . . Miss Maitland!

JEAN. Want to come along, girls?
(*Chorus.*)
BOBBY. Sure.
BERN. We'd love to.                                (*Simultaneously as girls*
TONY. Yes.                                         *go upstairs.*)

(*The whole procession streams toward stairs, talking as they go.*)

JEAN. I haven't heard a bit of Club news. What are you girls all doing? What's happened? Who's got jobs?
BIG M. I have. And Kendall's working. And Judy. And let's see—who else?
SUSAN. I'm understudy in " Roman Candle."
LITTLE M. You read about Linda, I suppose. Getting all smashed up?
JEAN. Oh, wasn't it ghastly!
BERN. And Kaye's taking poison. I suppose you know about that.
JEAN. Oh, I almost died.
BERN. That was awfully exciting. Pictures in the paper, and everything.
FRANK. (*Bringing up the rear with electrical apparatus.*) You-all usin' this upstairs too, ain't you?

(TERRY *and* JUDITH, *unable to face a second such scene, remain behind, with only the smiling portrait of* JEAN *as company. Their eyes meet understandingly. There goes* JEAN.)

TERRY. (*Blandly.*) You're not going to be in the—other pictures?
JUD. No, if I'm going to work as an extra I want my five dollars a day.
TERRY. (*Crosses to* R. *of table.*) I do hope I left my room looking sordid enough.
JUD. (L.) Say, what about that play they've got her doing? Do you suppose it's really something?
TERRY. Oh, it is. David Kingsley told me about it. He says it's a really fine and moving play.
JUD. (*A glance at portrait.*) Then why does he let her do it?
TERRY. He couldn't help it. They got it into their heads out on the Coast. It's Gretzl's idea. What do they care about the theatre? They think the stage is something to advertise pictures with.

87

JUD. Listen, Jean can't act. If the play's as good as all that, she'll kill it. It doesn't make sense!

TERRY. Now, Judy, haven't you learned not to ——

*(Of all people, KEITH suddenly appears in archway. Though he has been gone a year, he barges right in as though he had left only yesterday. His clothes represent an ingenious blending of the Hollywood style with his own Leftist tendencies. He still wears the sweater, but it is an imported one, the trousers are beautifully tailored, the shirt probably cost eighteen dollars, no necktie, and, of course, no hat.)*

KEITH. *(His voice heard in hallway. Enter up R. down to C.)* Where's Terry Randall? Oh, there you are!

TERRY. *(Rises.)* Why, hello, Keith!

JUD. Well, if it isn't the fatted calf!

KEITH. *(Surveying room. D. R. to table.)* God, a year hasn't made any difference in this dump! *(He casts an appraising eye over TERRY.)* What's the matter with you? You're thin and you've got no color.

TERRY. *(R. of table.)* Well, I haven't been having those hamburgers at Smitty's since you left.

KEITH. That reminds me, I haven't had any breakfast. *(He selects a pear from bowl of fruit on table R., L. end.)* Hope this is ripe. . . . Heh! What's her name out there? *(Shouting toward dining room.)* Bring me a cup of coffee! *(Finding pear too juicy for him.)* God! Give me your handkerchief, Terry.

TERRY. *(Coming around front of couch.)* You've got one.

KEITH. That's silk. *(Grabs hers.)*

TERRY. Well, Keith, tell us about yourself. Are you back from Hollywood for good?

KEITH. What do you mean? I'm going back there in three days. I've been working on a plan to put the whole studio on a commonwealth basis with the electricians right on a footing with the executives. But they won't have it.

TERRY. Who won't have it, the executives?

KEITH. The electricians! *(Finishing up pear.)*

TERRY. Well, anyway you look wonderful. All healthy and sunburned. And I never saw such beautiful trousers.

KEITH. *(Taking a last bite of the pear.)* You're looking terrible. *(The core of the pear in hand, he glances about for some place to deposit it. Lightning-fast, the perfect servant,* JUDITH *is by his side, offering a little ash tray which she gets from piano. He drops the pear-core on it without a word.)*

JUD. Thank you. *(Replacing tray on piano,* R. *end.)*

KEITH. *(Eases to* C.—*Suddenly he notices* JEAN'S *portrait.)* What's *this* chromo doing here?

TERRY. It's a little present from Cinderella.

KEITH. *(Back* R. C.*)* Those autograph hounds out there waiting for her?

JUD. *(Drops* D. L. C.*)* No, they want another glimpse of *you.*

KEITH. Did it ever occur to you that I didn't come here to see *you?*

JUD. You mean there's—no hope for me at all? *(Crushed, she goes into dining room,* L.*)*

TERRY. *(On* L. *arm of couch.)* Well, Keith! Give me an account of yourself. You've been gone a year—I hardly know what's happened to you.

KEITH. *(*L. C.*)* Why—I wrote you—didn't I?

TERRY. Oh, yes. A postcard from Palm Springs, showing the cactus by moonlight, and a telegram of congratulations for my opening in February, which arrived two days after we closed.

KEITH. I got mixed up.

TERRY. Keith, tell me—what do you mean you're only going to be here three days? Your year's up, isn't it?

KEITH. Yeh, but they wouldn't let me go. I had to sign up for another year.

TERRY. But, Keith, your plays! You *are* writing another play?

KEITH. Yes. Sure. I haven't written it yet, but I will this year.

TERRY. *(Rises, drops down front of couch.)* I see. I saw the picture you wrote—what was the name of it? " Loads of Love."

KEITH. *(Moves* D. *and* R.*)* Oh, did you see that? How'd you like it?

TERRY. Very amusing. Of course, Keith, the Masses got a little crowded out.

KEITH. Masses! It played to eighty million people. That's masses, isn't it?

TERRY. *(Sits couch.)* Yes. Yes, I guess I didn't get the idea.

KEITH. *(Sits* L. *of her.)* Now listen, Sweet. You know why I'm here, don't you?

TERRY. No, I don't, Keith.

KEITH. Well, look! You can't go stumbling around like this forever. You're not working, are you?

TERRY. Yes.

KEITH. You are? What in?

TERRY. The blouse department of R. H. Macy & Co.

KEITH. What! You're kidding.

TERRY. I have to live, Keith.

KEITH. Good God! Listen, darling. You spend years on Broadway and finish up in Macy's. And look at Jean! Two years in Hollywood and she's a star.

TERRY. They speed up everything in Hollywood. In two years you're a star; in four you're forgotten, and in six you're back in Sweden. (*Moves* U. L. *to piano.*)

KEITH. Not any more. (*Doorbell rings.*) That's the kind of reasoning that's kept you where you are! From now on I'm going to take charge of you. You're going to be —— (*He breaks off as* MATTIE *crosses through hall from* L. *to* R. *Moves* D. R.) There's always somebody coming into this place. It's like Grand Central Station.

KINGSLEY. (*Heard at door.*) Good morning, Mattie.

MATTIE. (*At door.*) 'Morning, Mr. Kingsley.

KINGS. (*Appearing in archway.*) Hello, Terry. (*As he sees* KEITH.) Well, hello, there!

KEITH. Hello.

TERRY. David! How nice to see you!

KINGS. (*Glancing at portrait.*) I see I missed the ceremony.

TERRY. They're still shooting up on Stage Six.

KINGS. No, thanks. I'm the official escort, but there are limits. . . . (*As he drops down to* KEITH.) How are you, Burgess? I heard you were coming back.

KEITH. How are you? (*Shaking hands.*)

KINGS. So you've served your year, h'm? Well, you're an exception. You've had the courage to quit when you said you would. Another year out there, and you'd have gone the way they all do. Never written a fine play again.

(*A moment of embarrassed silence.*)

TERRY. (*Rather nervously.*) Keith is going back to Hollywood for one more year.

KINGS. Oh, I didn't mean to ——

KEITH. It always amuses me to hear a fellow like you, who makes his living out of pictures, turn on Hollywood and attack it. If you feel that way about pictures why do you work in them?

TERRY. (D. L. C. *Hurriedly.*) Well, we can't always do what we want to, Keith. After all, you're working in Hollywood, and I'm selling blouses, and David Kingsley is ——

KINGS. (*Moves* L.) No, Terry. He's right. I shouldn't talk that way, and I don't very often. But I'm a little worked up this morning. I re-read Jean's play last night. (*Gesturing toward* JEAN'S *portrait.*) And I realized more than ever what a beautiful play it is. That's what's got me a little low. When they come into the theatre— when picture people take a really fine play and put a girl like Jean in it; when they use a play like this for camera fodder, that's more than I can stand. The theatre means too much to me.

KEITH. (*Moves* L.) All right! It's a fine play. And you notice it's Hollywood that's doing it.

TERRY. Oh, Keith, let's not get into an argument.

KEITH. It just shows how much you know about Hollywood. You're five years behind the times. They're *crazy* about fine things. Dickens and Shakespeare—they've got a whole staff digging them up.

TERRY. All right! Let's talk about something else.

KEITH. If you go to a dinner in Hollywood, what's the conversation! Books, and Art, and Politics! They never even mention pictures.

KINGS. I suppose they put that on the dinner invitation. Instead of R. S. V. P. it says: Don't Mention Pictures.

TERRY. (*Coming between them.*) Oh, what's got into you two? You're a picture man and you're yelling about the stage, and you're a playwright and you're howling about Hollywood!

KINGS. At least I'm honest about it! I work in pictures, but I don't pretend to like it.

KEITH. (TERRY *moves* L.) Who's pretending? I like it and I'm going back there. And what's more, I'm taking Terry with me.

KINGS. You're what?

TERRY. (*Below chair* L. C.) Keith, don't be absurd!

KEITH. It's time somebody took her in hand, and I'm going to do it. I'm going to marry her.

KINGS. Terry, you can't do that!

TERRY. (*Hopefully.*) Why not, David?

KINGS. I've told you why a hundred times. You belong in the theatre.

TERRY. So that's the reason? Yes, you certainly *have* told me a

91

hundred times. A thousand! I've had it with the soup and the meat and the coffee. Actress, actress, actress!

KINGS. Of course I've told you! Because you *are* an actress!

TERRY. And I've just realized why. Because you quit the theatre yourself, and you've been salving your own conscience by preaching theatre to me. That made you feel less guilty.

KINGS. Terry, that's not true.

TERRY. Oh, yes, it is! So true! How funny that I never thought of it before!

KEITH. (*Who has vastly enjoyed all this.*) Look, I've got to get out of here! (*To* KINGSLEY.) If you'll let me have just a moment. (*Moves* L. *to* TERRY.) When are we going to get married?

TERRY. (*In a deadly tone.*) When are we going to get married! We are going to get married, Mr. Burgess, when Hollywood to Dunsinane doth come. That's Shakespeare; *you* know—the fellow they're digging up out there.

KEITH. (*Stunned.*) Huh?

TERRY. It's too late, Keith. When you walked out on me a year ago, you walked out on yourself, too. That other Keith was cocksure and conceited, but he stood for something! What was it?— thunder and lightning and power and truth! Wasn't that what you said? And if you believe in something you've got to be willing to starve for it. Well, I believed in it, Keith. (*She moves* D. R. *between them and stands looking from one to the other.*) So I guess that leaves me just a young lady with a career. Or shall we say just a young lady! (*She turns and goes upstairs.*)

## CURTAIN

## ACT III

SCENE 2: *Same. It is midnight, and the room is in semi-darkness. There is a pool of light in the hall and on stairway from overhead chandelier and desk lamp. A little later, when the lights go on, we see that Bernhardt has given way to Jean Maitland.*

*After a moment of stillness there is the sound of the front door opening, and the* TWO MARYS *are heard coming home and starting upstairs.*

LITTLE M. Well, I didn't like either the play *or* the cast. And I thought Laura Wilcox was terrible.

BIG M. Of course she's terrible. You know how she got the part, don't you?

LITTLE M. Sure. Everybody on Broadway knows. The trouble with us is we've been hanging on to our virtue.

BIG M. Maybe *you* have.

(*They disappear upstairs. Somewhere in hallway a clock strikes twelve. Then door is heard to open again.*)

JUD. (*Off* R.) Well, good night. And thank you ever so much. (*Enters* R.)

MILH. (*Enters.*) Thank you. I certainly had one swell evening, all right.

JUD. Yes, so did I! What time is it? About two o'clock?

MILH. No, it's only twelve.

JUD. Oh, really? I guess my watch is fast.

MILH. Look, I'm going to be here all week. What are you doing to-morrow night?

JUD. Tomorrow? That's Tuesday.—Oh, that's my gymnasium night.

MILH. Well, how about Wednesday?

JUD. Wednesday? Oh, I've got friends coming in from Europe, on the *Mauretania*.

MILH. The *Mauretania*? I thought they took that off.

JUD. Did I say *Mauretania*? Ah—*Minnetonka*.

MILH. Well, I've got to see you before I go. Of course I'll be back next month.

JUD. Next month? Oh, I spend November in the Catskills. My hay fever.

MILH. Well, I'll call you anyway tomorrow, on a chance. (*Exit* R.)

JUD. Swell chance! (*Starts up stairs.*)

FRANK. (*Enters up* L. *Crosses to window* R.) 'Evening, Miss Judith. You in early, ain't you?

JUD. It may seem early to you. (*Exit up stairs.*)

(FRANK *turns out lamp. Crosses* L., *and doorbell rings. He goes to door.*)

FRANK. Who's there?

KINGS. (*Outside.*) Hello, Frank.

FRANK. (*A change of tone as he opens the door.*) Why, Mr. Kingsley!

KINGS. (*In hall.*) I hope we didn't wake you up, Frank. May we come in?

FRANK. Yessah, yessah. Pardon my shirtsleeves. I thought one of the young ladies forgot her key.

(KINGSLEY *and* ANOTHER MAN *have come into view. The stranger is a short thick-set man who carries himself with great authority in order to make up for his lack of stature. Instinct tells you that this is none other than* ADOLPH GRETZL *himself.*)

KINGS. We wouldn't have bothered you at this hour, but it's terribly important. We want to see Miss Randall.

FRANK. Miss Terry! Why, she goes to sleep early. She got to get up half-past seven.

KINGS. (*Gently turning* FRANK *around and starting him toward stairs.*) It's all right. Wake her up and ask her to come down. (*Drops over* L.)

FRANK. Yessah. You ge'men want to wait in here? (*He turns on light in living room, then goes upstairs.*)

GRETZL. (*Looking about with disfavor.*) I don't like the whole idea. A fine actress don't live in a place like this.

KINGS. But she *is* a fine actress, Mr. Gretzl.

GRETZL. (*Drops down* C.) It don't look right to me. Something tells me it's no good.

KINGS. (L. C.) Mr. Gretzl, you've had this play in rehearsal for almost two weeks now. And she can't make the grade. You've got to face it—Jean is a motion picture actress. And that's all.

GRETZL. But she is a beautiful girl. When she comes on the stage people will gasp.

KINGS. You saw that rehearsal tonight. And that's the best she'll ever do.

GRETZL. But she's Jean Maitland! People will come to see Jean Maitland.

KINGS. (*Eases* L. *a bit.*) No, they won't. Theatre-goers won't come to see movie stars just because they're movie stars. They've got to act.

FRANK. (*Comes downstairs.*) Ah woke Miss Terry up. She's comin' right down. (*Goes down hall off up* L.)

KINGS. Thank you, Frank. . . . (*Points a stern finger toward head of stairs.*) Believe me, this girl's an actress.

GRETZL. All right, all right—an actress. Let's see her.

KINGS. (*Crosses R. Puts hat and coat on table.*) She's got presence and authority and distinction! And a beautiful mobile face. She's exactly right for this play.

GRETZL. (*In front of couch.*) If she is such a great beauty and such a wonderful actress, where's she been keeping herself?

KINGS. She's been learning her business.

GRETZL. (*Crosses L.*) All right, we'll let her read the part. What else am I here for in the middle of the night? She's got to start tomorrow morning—tonight, even. It's a great big part. Everything depends on it.

KINGS. (*Over R.*) She can do it. She's young and eager and fresh. Wait till you see her. (TERRY *comes downstairs, wearing a loose flowing robe over her long white nightgown. Her hair is loose on her shoulders. Her feet are in low scuffs. She is anything but the dazzling figure described by* KINGSLEY. *She comes into the room wordlessly, looking at the two men.* KINGSLEY, *going to meet her* c.) It's sweet of you to come down, Terry. I wasn't sure you would.

TERRY. You knew I would, David.

KINGS. Terry, this is Mr. Gretzl. This is Terry Randall.

TERRY. How do you do, Mr. Gretzl?

(GRETZL *mumbles a greeting,* "*How do you do?*")

KINGS. Terry, I suppose I needn't tell you why we're here at this hour. Could you start rehearsing tomorrow morning in this play of Mr. Gretzl's, and open in a week?

GRETZL. Wait a minute, Kingsley. Not so fast, there! Let me look at her. (*He slowly describes a half-circle around her, his eyes intent on her face. As the inspection finishes she turns her head and meets his gaze. But* GRETZL'S *inquiring look is now directed at* KINGSLEY.) This is the party you just now described to me?

KINGS. (*Crossing* GRETZL *to* TERRY. *Pulling a typed* "*part*" *out of his pocket.*) Terry, I know what you can do, but Mr. Gretzl doesn't. Will you read a couple of speeches of this—let him hear you?

TERRY. (*A little terrified at the thought.*) Now?

KINGS. Would you, Terry?

TERRY. I'll try.

KINGS. (*Giving her the part.*) How about this bit here?

TERRY. May I look at it a second, just to ——?

KINGS. Of course. (*Turns to* GRETZL.) You know, it's rather difficult to jump right into a character.

GRETZL. (*Crossing* L. *to armchair.*) What's difficult! We do it every day in pictures. . . . Come on, young lady. Well —— (*He turns a chair around, seats himself ostentatiously, and beckons* TERRY *to stand directly in front of him and perform.*)

TERRY. (*A deep sigh, takes the plunge. Reads:*) "Look, boys, I haven't got any right to stand up here and tell you what to do. Only maybe I have got a right, see, because, look ——" No, that isn't right. "Because, look ——" Do you mind if I start all over?

GRETZL. (*Annoyed.*) All right, go ahead. Start over. (*Gets cigar from pocket.*)

TERRY. (*To* KINGSLEY.) What's she want them to do?

KINGS. Strike. (*Sits* L. *arm of couch.*)

TERRY. Oh. Uh —— (*She is off again, less certain of herself than ever.*) "Look, boys ——" (*A bad start again,* GRETZL *spits out end of cigar he has bitten off, but she quickly recovers herself.*) "Look, boys, I haven't got any right to stand up here and tell you what to do. Only maybe I have got a right, see, because, look, I'm engaged to be married. You all know who it is. He's right here in this hall." (GRETZL *rises abruptly and up to piano for match.* TERRY *goes on stumblingly.*) " —in this hall. So if you fellas vote to go on strike, why, I guess it's no wedding bells for me. Don't kid yourself I don't know what I'm talking about. Because I've been through it before. I've been through it with my old man, and my brothers, so I ought to know." (GRETZL *has picked up a match-box from piano, and now strikes a match with a sharp rasping sound and lights a long cigar.*) "It means hungry, and maybe cold, and scared every minute somebody'll come home with a busted head. But which would you ruther do? Die quick fighting, or starve to death slow! That's why I'm telling you—strike! strike! Strike!" (GRETZL *has again seated himself in front of her, and as he throws back his head, the better to survey her, a cloud of cigar-smoke is blown upward toward her face.*) "That's why I'm telling you— strike! Strike! S ——" (*She has been choking back a cough, but it now becomes too much for her. She stops and throws part to floor. Tears and anger struggle for mastery.*) I can't do it! I can't! I won't go on!

KINGS. (*Rising. Angered.*) You're a fool if you do.

GRETZL. (*Rising and buttoning his coat with a gesture of finality. Crosses to couch, gets his hat.*) You must excuse me. I am a plain-speaking man. I don't want to hurt anybody's feelings, but in my opinion this young lady is not anything at all. Not anything.

TERRY. (*To GRETZL.*) But, Mr. Gretzl, nobody could give a reading under these conditions. It isn't fair. It isn't possible for an actress —you don't understand.

GRETZL. All right. I don't understand. But I understand my business and I know what I see. So I will say good night, and thank you. Come on, Kingsley.

KINGS. I'm sorry, Terry. No one could look a great actress in bathrobe and slippers, and Mr. Gretzl only knows what he sees.

GRETZL. Are you working for me or against me, Kingsley?

KINGS. I'm working *for* you. What are you going to do about your play tomorrow?

GRETZL. I'm going to throw it into the ash-can. All I wanted it for was Jean Maitland. So she could make a picture of it. All right. She does something else. I can get plenty material.

KINGS. It's incredible that anyone should be so stupid.

GRETZL. (*Rising to his full height.*) Mr. Kingsley, you are *out*. You will hear from our lawyers in the morning. (*Starts up.*)

TERRY. Oh, David!

KINGS. (*After GRETZL. Both stop C. in hall.*) It's all right, Terry. Gretzl, if you've lost your interest in the play, how about selling it to me?

GRETZL. I see. You're going back into the theatre, eh?

KINGS. I might. Will you sell it to me?

GRETZL. How much?

KINGS. Just what it cost you.

GRETZL. All right. See Becker in the morning. He'll fix it up. Good night.

KINGS. Good night.

GRETZL. (*As he goes.*) And I am the stupid one, huh! (*Exits up R.*)

TERRY. David, David, oh, my dear, you mustn't do this just for me.

KINGS. (*Drops down L. C. to her.*) No, I'm not one of those boys who puts on a play just so that his girl can act in it. . . . By the way, you *are* my girl, aren't you?

TERRY. (*Brightly.*) Oh, yes, sir.

KINGS. I just thought I'd ask. (*Kisses her.*) You know I had a couple of pretty nasty weeks, since you drove me out into the cold.

TERRY. Weeks? It seemed like years to me.

(*Another embrace.* MRS. ORCUTT *enters in dressing-gown and slippers.*)

MRS. OR. I'm sorry, Mr. Kingsley, but this is against the rules.
TERRY. Mrs. Orcutt, it's the play!
KINGS. My apologies, Mrs. Orcutt. This may look a little strange. But I came up on business.
MRS. OR. Frank said there was another gentleman.
TERRY. (*Gaily.*) But he's gone! And, oh, Mrs. Orcutt! I'm going to do the play! (*At the end of this announcement, as she says "play," her hand goes to her mouth, like a little girl's, she is surprised to find herself crying in* KINGSLEY'S *arms.*)
MRS. OR. Terry, my child!
KINGS. Darling, you're tired. You must get your sleep. (*There is a farewell kiss, with the full approval of* MRS. ORCUTT.) Good night. (*He picks up part where* TERRY *has thrown it. Hands it to her and gets hat and coat from table* R.)
TERRY. Good night.
KINGS. (*Starting for hall.*) Eleven in the morning, at the Music Box.
TERRY. (*In a low voice.*) I'll be there.

(KINGSLEY *is gone off up* R.)

MRS. OR. Terry, dear, I'm so happy for you. Aren't you thrilled?
TERRY. It was like Victoria. When they came to tell her she was Queen.
MRS. OR. Dear child! But now you must run along to bed and get some sleep.
TERRY. No, no. I must learn my part. And I must be alone. I want a room by myself tonight. Please, Mrs. Orcutt.
MRS. OR. I'll see what I can do. (*She goes, first switching off main light, exit up* L.)

(TERRY *stands alone in the semi-darkened room. A light from a street-lamp shines through the window and strikes her face. For a moment she stands perfectly still. Then the realization of her new position comes over her. She seems to take on height and dignity.*)

98

TERRY. Now that I am the Queen, I wish in future to have a bed, and a room, of my own. (*She stands transfixed as the curtain falls.*)

## CURTAIN

# PROPERTY PLOT

## ACT I—SCENE 1

Bust of Shakespeare on c. of mantel.
Ash trays on mantel and small table.
Large portrait of Bernhardt over mantel.
Bowl of flowers on piano.
Ash tray on piano.
Magazine on piano.
Writing materials on desk.
Ash tray on desk.
Theatrical mementoes such as a shoe, dagger, etc., on shelves of desk.
Ash trays on table.
Magazines on table.
Letters on top of R. arch.
3 books on L. arch

On table in dining room
{
6 places set
Doilies
Service plates
Soup dishes
Covered vegetable dish, butter dish
Cutlery
Glasses
Ash trays
}

### PROPS OFF STAGE L.

1 clock gong.

### PROPS ON PLATFORM OFF STAGE

3 ladies' bags: 1 large, 1 small, 1 hat box.
Towels: 4 hand, 2 bath.
Girl's wrist-watch (Louise).
Magazine on table.

## ACT I—SCENE 2

### BEDROOM

On Dresser over R. (TERRY'S):
  1 black night eyeshade.
  1 ash tray.
  1 vanity box with mirror (to reflect light on Kaye's bed).

1 black comb.
1 black brush.
2 photographs.
1 program.
2 or 3 telegrams stuck in wall mirror.
Snapshots stuck in wall mirror.
Perfume bottle.
Jar of cold cream.
Hand towel.
Frowners (in drawer)
Kleenex (in drawer).
On Dresser up R. (JEAN'S):
  2 photos of picture actresses.
  Manicure set.
  Glass powder jar.
  Glass perfume bottle.
  Comb and brush.
  1 small alarm clock.
On Dresser up L. (KAYE'S)
  Comb and brush.
  1 nail file.
  1 buffer.
  Bottle of perfume.
  A program
  1 black night eyeshade.
  1 curling iron.
  1 pocketbook in drawer; about $2.60 in it.
  1 pair black cotton gloves.
  1 pin cushion with threaded needle.
  1 small vase of flowers.
  1 piece of pink ribbon.
Lingerie and stockings thrown over Kaye's chair up L.
Pair of carpet slippers foot of Terry's bed.

## OFF STAGE L.

Towel }
Comb } For Kaye.

## ACT II—SCENE 1

Change magazines.
1 pink letter with mail (Bobby).
1 blue letter with mail (Terry).
Carpet-sweeper by armchair (Frank).
Newspaper over back of armchair (Frank).
Vase of long-stemmed flowers on table R.

Clock gong.
Cup of coffee.
Newspaper.
Lipstick (Ann).
Dustcloth ⎫
Ash receptacle ⎬ Mattie.

Cigarettes
Matches
Keith.
Letter (Dr. Randall).

2 typewritten pages radio manuscript (Terry).
A manuscript part (Little Mary).
Money (Linda).
Small overnight bag (Linda).
Music portfolio (Olga).

### ACT II—SCENE 2

Gold cigarette case (Keith).

1 banana (Judith).

### ACT III—SCENE 1

1 bowl of fruit with pear for Keith and apple for Madeleine on table R.
1 roll R. end of table.

7 coffee cups ⎰ 1 on L. arch by telephone
1 on R. end of piano
1 under piano
1 D. L. for Big Mary
1 D. L. C. for Ellen
1 D. R. C. for Madeleine
1 on R. end of table

Sunday newspapers:
    Comic section of tabloid on rail arch L. for Bobby.
    News section of paper on piano for Pat.
    Magazine section of newspaper D. L. for Big Mary.
    Section of tabloid on floor by chair L. C. (Mirror).
    Section of the news for Judith in armchair L. C.
    Advertising section of newspaper on floor above chair L. C. for Ellen.

102

Rotogravure section for Madeleine D. R. C.
Dramatic section of newspaper on couch R. for Kendall.
News section newspaper on floor near couch for Kendall.
News section on floor L. of table for Susan.
Section of newspaper R. C. on floor for Louise.
1 banana—Little Mary.
1 apple—Judith.
½ grapefruit on head of Shakespeare bust.
1 large ash tray R. end of piano.
1 letter for Judith.

OFF STAGE R.

Large view camera on tripod.
1 photo flood lamp.
Large framed portrait draped with red velvet (Jean).

OFF STAGE L.

Large serving tray (Mattie).
Cup of coffee.
Spoon.

ACT III—SCENE 2

Change picture of Bernhardt to Jean Maitland.
Ash tray with matches on piano.
Manuscript part (Kingsley).
Cigar (Gretzl).
Watch (Judith).

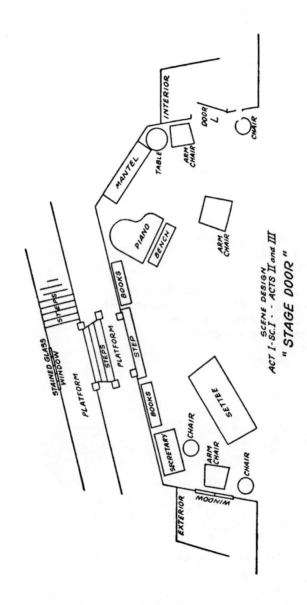

SCENE DESIGN
ACT I - SC.I - ACTS II and III

"STAGE DOOR"

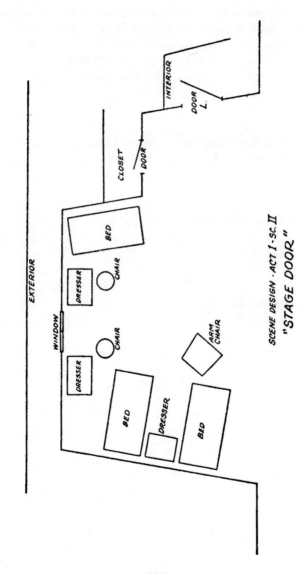

SCENE DESIGN - ACT 1 - SC. II
"STAGE DOOR"

*Textual changes to be made in the published version of* Stage Door *enabling groups to produce the play in a single interior set. Additional cuts indicated render staging easier and exclude two characters and occasional dialogue which may be considered a little too "advanced" for the average high school. These instructions are to be used in connection with the printed text of* Stage Door.

**Cast of Character Page:** Omit names of Linda Shaw and Mrs. Shaw. Same page substitute for present list of scenes the following only: "the scene is the main room of the Footlights Club, somewhere in the West 50s, New York City."

**Page 5:** Omit reference to Bernhardt portrait. Toward bottom of page omit 3 1/2 lines beginning, "Two girls are" and ending with "sultry look-ing." Same page, a little further on, omit lines beginning, "for a moment" and ending in F Minor." Also omit last line on page, "The piano again."

**Page 6:** Cut first 9 lines. (NOTE: Piano has been cut from these stage directions, and all references to playing. If practical to have piano on stage and someone can play it well, disregard these cuts. However, if piano can be used off stage, make such changes as will permit music to be heard). Same page: cut last line on page.

**Page 7:** Toward bottom of page omit stage direction, "Olga starts playing again."

**Page 8:** Cut stage direction, "continues playing."

**Page 9:** A little below center of page cut stage direction, "then raises her voice," and cut the rest of that speech.

**Page 10:** Toward bottom of page Mrs. Orcutt's speech after "I under-stand," cut next 7 lines and begin, "I try very hard..."

**Page 11:** Cut everything between stage directions "Down the stairs" and next to last line on page.

**Page 13:** Cut Mary's line a little below middle of the page, "she is oversexed!"

**Page 14:** Cut from Judith's speech a little below middle of page the words, "the Hell." Same page, last line on page, cut stage direction beginning "Linda" (which goes through to page 15, middle of the third line from top) ending "Up stairs."

**Page 18:** Judith's speech below middle of page cut line, "We don't want to give him the wrong idea of this house."

**Page 19:** Jean's speech toward bottom of page substitute "Bathroom" for "Johnny."

**Page 24:** Beginning with 9th line from the top, beginning Ann's speech, cut everything on page.

**Page 25:** Cut entire page down to 3rd line from bottom beginning "A man's voice at door." Keep in this last sentence.

**Page 26:** 8th line from top of page cut entire page beginning, "Bernice comes out of dining room."

**Page 27:** Cut first 4 lines on page and 5th line up to mention of Mrs. Orcutt. 2 lines below add the words, "Appears from the dining room" after the word, "gown."

**Page 28:** 13 lines from bottom substitute "Soul's my own," for "Soul belongs to God."

**Page 29:** 11th line cut sentence beginning "Mother used to say." Cut Terry's line middle of page reading, "Oh, I hope I didn't."

**Page 30:** 12 lines from bottom change "Goddamn" to "darn."

**Page 33:** Last speech in scene. Substitute "Heck's" for Hell's." Omit last 2 lines of stage directions in this scene.

(NOTE FOLLOWING CHANGE IN STAGE DIRECTIONS AND ARRANGEMENTS FOR ACT 1, SCENE 2: Because of the rearrangements suggested it is not necessary to have a separate bedroom for the scene. It will be noted that Kaye waits in a bathrobe for Terry as Judith does in a housecoat. Terry wears ordinary clothes. Judith exits as indicated and Terry and Kaye exit to stairs as Jean enters. Jean exits on curtain. Cut last 8 lines of stage directions on page.)

**Page 34.** Cut lines 14 and 15. Cut lines 21 through 26. In Judith's speech at bottom of page cut the words "The rest of us are always spilling our whole insides, but,"

**Page 35:** Cut first 10 lines on page. Cut lines 17 through 31.

**Page 36:** Top line cut beginning, "I've got" through the 7th line ending "delinquent girls." 6th line from bottom change "damned" to "darned."

**Page 37:** Cut last 18 lines on page.

**Page 38:** 14 lines from top cut short stage direction beginning, "She is pulling."

**Page 39:** Cut last 3 lines on page and all of the 4th line from bottom except the word "to."

**Page 40:** Cut first 23 lines. 10th line from bottom change word, "downstairs" to "down here". Cut last line on page.

**Page 41:** Cut first 13 lines. To line 17 add stage direction, "They exit upstairs together." At the end of stage direction on line 20 add stage direction, "Kaye goes upstairs again." 4th line from bottom omit Kaye's speech, "Oh girls, how exciting."

**Page 45:** Omit lines 5 through 8. In line 12 substitute, "We" for "The nuns." From Judith's speech in middle of page omit, "Maybe it's a little stranger. She's been married a year."

**Page 47:** 13th line from top substitute "Shakespeare" for "The Passion Play". 4 lines below substitute "cute" for "like a cutie."

**Page 48:** 5th line from top add word "script" too "radio." 12th line from top substitute "heck" for "Hell."

**Page 50:** Cut last 8 lines on page.

**Page 51:** Cut entire page.

**Page 52:** Ditto.

**Page 53:** Ditto.

**Page 54:** Cut first line, all except last 3 words. On line 6 cut everything after word, "music." Cut everything from line 7 through line 21. On lines 22 and 23 omit "Chopin B Minor Etude Op. 25, No. 40."

**Page 59:** 14th line from bottom, substitute "swell" for "hell of an." 5 lines from bottom substitute "gosh" for "God".

**Page 60:** Omit lines 3 through 20. Line 22, substitute "great" for "hell of a." Line 25, substitute "Pete's" for "God's."

**Page 61:** 21st line from top add to Kaye's speech "for everything." 27th line from top after Terry's "Yes" add stage direction, "preoccupiedly looking upstairs." Omit last 9 lines on page. Curtain descends after stage direction, "Door slams."

**Page 62:** Omit entire page.

**Page 63:** 2 lines from bottom substitute "Heavens" for "Lord."

**Page 64:** 3rd line from top change, "Miss Kendall's room," to "your room, girls."

**Page 66:** Change "damnedest" to "darndist," in 5th line from top.

**Page 71:** 3rd line from bottom substitute "The important thing" for "all."

**Page 73:** 12th line from bottom substitute "Oh yeah" for "The hell you can't." 5th line from bottom omit sentence, "It's good old sex appeal."

Omit last 3 lines on page.

**Page 74:** Cut first 6 lines on page. Line 10 from top omit "Chopin's C Sharp Minor Waltz" and substitute word "playing." 3rd line from bottom of page omit "God." Omit last 6 words on page.

**Page 75:** Omit first 2 lines. Omit 4th and 5th lines from top.

**Page 76:** Omit first 6 lines and word, "Yes," in 7th line.

**Page 77:** Omit lines 11 and 12, 14 and 15 from top. In line 17 omit word "Besides." Omit 3rd and 4th lines from bottom of page.

**Page 84:** Omit last 4 lines on page and all of the 5th line except words, "Oh fine."

**Page 85:** Omit entire page except last 4 lines.

**Page 86:** In 1st and 2nd lines from top omit the words "behind the portrait." Larry's speech, middle of page, substitute "her" for "em."

**Page 87:** Omit lines 13, 14 and 15, one speech read by Mary and Jean. In Bernice's speech omit "taking poison" and substitute "tragic death."

**Page 88:** 15th line from top of page omit "God." 15th line from bottom of page omit "God."

**Page 90:** 6th line from top of page omit "Good God." 17th line from bottom of page omit stage direction, "glancing at portrait," and change word "ceremony" to "welcome."

# NEW PLAYS

★ **INTIMATE APPAREL by Lynn Nottage.** The moving and lyrical story of a turn-of-the-century black seamstress whose gifted hands and sewing machine are the tools she uses to fashion her dreams from the whole cloth of her life's experiences. "…Nottage's play has a delicacy and eloquence that seem absolutely right for the time she is depicting…" *–NY Daily News.* "…thoughtful, affecting…The play offers poignant commentary on an era when the cut and color of one's dress—and of course, skin—determined whom one could and could not marry, sleep with, even talk to in public." *–Variety.* [2M, 4W] ISBN: 0-8222-2009-1

★ **BROOKLYN BOY by Donald Margulies.** A witty and insightful look at what happens to a writer when his novel hits the bestseller list. "The characters are beautifully drawn, the dialogue sparkles…" *–nytheatre.com.* "Few playwrights have the mastery to smartly investigate so much through a laugh-out-loud comedy that combines the vintage subject matter of successful writer-returning-to-ethnic-roots with the familiar mid-life crisis." *–Show Business Weekly.* [4M, 3W] ISBN: 0-8222-2074-1

★ **CROWNS by Regina Taylor.** Hats become a springboard for an exploration of black history and identity in this celebratory musical play. "Taylor pulls off a Hat Trick: She scores thrice, turning CROWNS into an artful amalgamation of oral history, fashion show, and musical theater…" *–TheatreMania.com.* "…wholly theatrical…Ms. Taylor has created a show that seems to arise out of spontaneous combustion, as if a bevy of department-store customers simultaneously decided to stage a revival meeting in the changing room." *–NY Times.* [1M, 6W (2 musicians)] ISBN: 0-8222-1963-8

★ **EXITS AND ENTRANCES by Athol Fugard.** The story of a relationship between a young playwright on the threshold of his career and an aging actor who has reached the end of his. "[Fugard] can say more with a single line than most playwrights convey in an entire script…Paraphrasing the title, it's safe to say this drama, making its memorable entrance into our consciousness, is unlikely to exit as long as a theater exists for exceptional work." *–Variety.* "A thought-provoking, elegant and engrossing new play…" *–Hollywood Reporter.* [2M] ISBN: 0-8222-2041-5

★ **BUG by Tracy Letts.** A thriller featuring a pair of star-crossed lovers in an Oklahoma City motel facing a bug invasion, paranoia, conspiracy theories and twisted psychological motives. "…obscenely exciting…top-flight craftsmanship. Buckle up and brace yourself…" *–NY Times.* "…[a] thoroughly outrageous and thoroughly entertaining play…the possibility of enemies, real and imagined, to squash has never been more theatrical." *–A.P.* [3M, 2W] ISBN: 0-8222-2016-4

★ **THOM PAIN (BASED ON NOTHING) by Will Eno.** An ordinary man muses on childhood, yearning, disappointment and loss, as he draws the audience into his last-ditch plea for empathy and enlightenment. "It's one of those treasured nights in the theater—treasured nights anywhere, for that matter—that can leave you both breathless with exhilaration and…in a puddle of tears." *–NY Times.* "Eno's words…are familiar, but proffered in a way that is constantly contradictory to our expectations. Beckett is certainly among his literary ancestors." *–nytheatre.com.* [1M] ISBN: 0-8222-2076-8

★ **THE LONG CHRISTMAS RIDE HOME by Paula Vogel.** Past, present and future collide on a snowy Christmas Eve for a troubled family of five. "…[a] lovely and hauntingly original family drama…a work that breathes so much life into the theater." *–Time Out.* "…[a] delicate visual feast…" *–NY Times.* "…brutal and lovely…the overall effect is magical." *–NY Newsday.* [3M, 3W] ISBN: 0-8222-2003-2

**DRAMATISTS PLAY SERVICE, INC.**
**440 Park Avenue South, New York, NY 10016  212-683-8960  Fax 212-213-1539**
**postmaster@dramatists.com  www.dramatists.com**